"Dick Armstrong has been a friend and inspiration to me for decades. I thought I knew Dick, but now I really know him after reading *A Sense of Being Called*. This book will stir your soul and lift your spirit just as it has done for me."

—PAT WILLIAMS
Senior Vice President, Orlando Magic

"This is a true 'I can't wait to hear what's next' story. It's a fascinating account of how God called a young Major League baseball front office executive into the ministry. Dick Armstrong had never thought of becoming a minister. What he calls his 'Damascus Road' experience was the most direct and unexpected call I have ever heard of, and anyone who reads this book will have a renewed appreciation of the miraculous ways God works in people's lives. This beautifully told story would make a wonderful text for any book club or church study group, and I can testify that it will evoke a range of emotions—from tears to chuckles, from being informed about a profession not many people know about, to being inspired by a young man's unanticipated pilgrimage of faith."

—SAMUEL H. MOFFETT
Professor of Ecumenics and Mission Emeritus, Princeton Theological Seminary

"Spring training is a busy time for baseball clubs. A veteran of those days of warmth and pre-season hopes, Dick Armstrong tells of his years as the public relations director of the Baltimore Orioles and how his life changed one evening in Florida, when he was unexpectedly confronted with a call from God. Those who read his deeply personal narration of this dramatic encounter and the events that followed will themselves be confronted with what it means to be called by God. This book is a stirring challenge to think about the difference between choosing a career and being called by God to follow a path in life. Armstrong's call is one that can speak not just to those who know God, but to those who barely do or are not sure they do. It is a must read!"

—KATHY J. NELSON
President, F.I.S.H. (Funding Individual Spiritual Health) Foundation, Inc.

A Sense of Being *Called*

Warmest regards to my dear friend Barbara, whom I have known and admired for many, many years!

Dick

A Sense of Being
Called

Richard Stoll Armstrong

CASCADE *Books* · Eugene, Oregon

A SENSE OF BEING CALLED

Cascade Books
An Imprint of Wipf and Stock Publishers
199 W. 8th Ave., Suite 3
Eugene, OR 97401

www.wipfandstock.com

ISBN 13: 978-1-60899-404-5

Cataloging-in-Publication data

Armstrong, Richard Stoll, 1924–.

A sense of being called / Richard Stoll Armstrong.

xvi + 192 p. ; 23 cm.

ISBN 13: 978-1-60899-404-5

1. Clergy—Office. 2. Christian leadership. 3. Presbyterian Church—United States—Biography. I. Title.

BV4011.3 .A76 2011

Manufactured in the U.S.A.

To my wife, Margie;

our parents,

Willa and Harwood Childs

Elsie and Herb Armstrong;

our five children,

Ellen, Ricky, Andy, Woody, and Elsie;

the many other beautiful people

who were part of this story;

and to God,

who made it all possible

Contents

Shibe Park was renamed Connie Mack Stadium in 1953. The press box was male turf in those days.

Preface

For the Boys in the Press Box

At the urging of my family and of others who are familiar with fragments of my pilgrimage from the press box to the pulpit, I have finally decided to put the story down on paper.

I do so not because it tells anything remarkable about me, but because it shows how remarkable God is. My call to the ministry of the gospel is a tribute to the reality of a personal God who can call the most unlikely and unsuspecting persons into his service, and who guides, provides for, and equips those whom he calls, in the most amazing ways.

In short, it is God's story, not mine. As human instruments in God's story, however, we can also speak of our story not as *the* story but as *a* story, which points to the God who makes it possible. My call, as it turned out, was to become an ordained minister. It is important for people to understand that God calls people in different ways, to different roles, and for different tasks. All of us who profess to believe in Jesus Christ are called to be stewards, and witnesses, and worshipers, and reconcilers. Jesus bids us to take up a cross daily and follow him (Luke 9:23; cf., Matt 16:24; Mark 8:34). Each of us should be continually asking, What is God calling me to be or to do? When one has a sense of call, it is always a story worth telling.

Many times over the years I have been asked how I happened to leave professional baseball to go into the ministry. Some parts of the story are indelibly engraved on my heart while other parts have faded from memory with the passage of time. In this Lucan attempt to set down an orderly account of the events of this part of my life, I have found that memory often plays tricks with the facts. What I have written differs in some minor respects from the way I had recalled and have been telling the story. What follows in these pages is what really took place.

This is a story, not an academic dissertation on the theology of the call of God. That's because I want readers to walk with me on my faith pilgrimage, and to experience what I was thinking and feeling as the events unfolded. The events are described and interpreted as I experienced them at the time. I deliberately did not want to inject my present theological perspective into the narrative. Instead I wanted to share the insights as they came to me along the way, thus revealing my own faith development and allowing the reader to share in the discovery process.

It is crucial to understanding my sense of call that initially I saw no connection whatsoever between my son's illness and my Damascus Road experience. That awareness came much later. Had I suspected a connection, I would have questioned my motives and probably would not be in the ministry today. The point is that God knew that about me, and hence did not give me that insight until, with the hindsight of my growing faith and understanding, I was ready for it.

I want this narrative to be a strong and positive witness to the grace of God, who is able to work miracles in people's lives, even the most unlikely ones, like me. I'm hoping to reach the kinds of people who normally would never look at a theological textbook, like most of "the boys" I knew in the press box. I say "boys" because there were no "gals" in the press box back in those days. The press box was male turf, and that's where I spent most of my time during the games that my friends were covering or broadcasting.

This book is written for them, although few if any of them are still around to read it. They were all older than I was then, and religion was never something we talked about. That is not to say that many of them were not believers; they just didn't talk about it. After I became a minister, however, I was surprised at how many of them were interested or curious to hear how it had happened.

Over the years I've told parts of the story countless times. This is the first time I have attempted to recount the entire story of my journey from baseball to the ministry. The conversations and direct quotations in this book are as close to verbatim as memory allows. The tone and substance are consistently accurate, even when the wording may not be exact. To fix the dates, times, and circumstances of the events I shall be relating I have not had to rely on my ability to recall long-forgotten details. Fortunately, I have years of correspondence with family and friends to draw upon. My wife, Margie, and I saved all the letters we ever received from our parents, as they did ours. We reacquired those letters after our parents died, and we also have every letter we ever wrote to each other. All these, along with other correspondence, calendars, diaries, pictures, home movies, and newspaper clippings we have saved, have proven to be an invaluable resource, enabling me to put the details of this historical account in their proper sequence and context. In such a project as this, it pays to be a pack rat!

Most of this story has never been told. When I have been asked to share parts of it publicly, I have done so with the hope that others will be encouraged to think about and to share their own stories. For everyone has a story to tell, and to the extent that one's story points to the amazing grace of God, it will always be a powerful testimony.

The way I was called into ministry is not the way it usually happens. In a survey of ministerial candidates conducted during my middler year in seminary I was one of only two students out of the 888 respondents who indicated that their call was unmistakable from the first! Fewer than 5 percent reported a sudden, dramatic call into the ministry and could pinpoint the time and place it happened. For the vast majority the call was the result of a gradual process, usually over a period of several years.

I have always stressed, and I want to do so here, that those who read this story should not think that the kind of experience I had is necessary in order to know that one has been called by God. What happened to me is not typical, and others who have not had such an experience should not feel as if they are missing something.

Some people have mistakenly referred to what happened to me as a conversion. Although I speak of it as my Damascus Road experience (see Acts 9, 22, and 26), it was not a conversion in the true sense. I was already a believer. In fact, I cannot remember a time when I did not believe in God, nor can I possibly name the date when I first believed. I have always believed in God.

But I can pinpoint the time and place when and where I was called to be a minister. I suppose that could be called a *vocational* conversion. It was also the beginning of a totally new and dramatically different relationship with the God in whom I had always believed, but who had never encountered me in such a powerfully transforming way. If God had been calling me before that, I was not aware of it. Perhaps God had been trying to reach me for years, but I was not listening. It took a Damascus Road experience to get my attention!

Some who read this story may readily identify with it. They and I are standing on common ground, and for that I am grateful and happy. Others, however, may feel they are traveling through unfamiliar territory. I hope my experience will encourage them to think about the ways in which God has already been at work in their lives and to be open to new, life-changing encounters.

Still others may be skeptical and even cynical about my speaking of a personal God who can intervene in people's lives in such mysterious and wonderful ways. Such a person would probably not be reading a book like this, but if one did, that person would reject the obvious assumptions upon which the story is based. The difference between a believer and a nonbeliever is a matter of who gets the credit. Nonbelievers attribute the remarkable things that happen to circumstance, coincidence, or chance. Believers give the credit to God.

Since I admit that my testimony is an affirmation of faith, my experience confirms for me the truth of that affirmation. That is why I am writing this story. It is not offered as a proof for the existence of God, but as confirming evidence of the reality of God for those who already believe.

Many of the individuals who were part of the story are no longer alive, including especially Margie's and my parents and our son Ricky. Would that they were here to receive my expression of gratitude for the roles they played in my journey of faith. Others who are still around may be surprised to see their names mentioned in this story. I want to thank them, too!

But I especially want to thank my wonderful wife, Margie, who has been so helpful not only in recalling names, places, and events but also in encouraging me to get started at long last on this project, and to keep going, when at times I have been tempted to give it up.

R. S. A.
Princeton, New Jersey

Acknowledgments

Most of the photographs used in this book have been in my possession for fifty years or more. Many were snapshots taken by me or by a family member. The picture of old Oriole Park is from a Wikipedia article and is used in accordance with Wikipedia's Creative Commons Attribution-ShareAlike Unported 3.0 License. The autographed pictures of Yogi Berra and Mickey Mantle were a gift to my son from the then-public relations director of the New York Yankees.

All the pictures of Philadelphia Athletics' and Baltimore Orioles' personalities are from my personal files, taken either by the club photographer or by someone who can no longer be identified. One exception is the picture of Herb Armstrong with Judge Landis, which was taken in 1923 by *Baltimore Sun* photographer Leroy Merriken. Some of the press photographers were my good friends and I am indebted to all of them for their many kindnesses.

I also want to thank Cynthia Ballard for the picture of her husband, Wilson; Sandy Vrooman McCormick and Skip Vrooman for the picture of their father, Terry Vrooman; Andy Glen for the picture of his grandparents, Betty and Len Bauer; and the Communications/Publications Department of Princeton Theological Seminary for the use of the photographs of some of the professors and campus buildings.

And last but certainly not least, I should like to express my deep gratitude to Dr. K. C. Hanson, Christian Amondson, and the entire Wipf and Stock team for their tremendous expertise and wonderful cooperation in bringing this project to a successful conclusion.

Prologue

Convocation Day

"I want to extend the sympathy of the seminary community to one of our new students and his wife following the death of their child early this morning . . ."

The voice was that of Dr. John A. Mackay, president of Princeton Theological Seminary, who was delivering his welcoming remarks at the convocation of the New Jersey seminary's 144th year. The child to whom he referred was our five-and-a-half-year-old son, Ricky.

Miller Chapel was packed that night. My wife, Margie, had persuaded me to attend the service, thinking it might help somewhat to ease the pain. Agreeing that I needed an antidote for the emotions flooding my heart, I had decided at the last moment to attend the service. Having had no sleep at all the night before, I felt like a zombie, as I sat near the back of that lovely colonial sanctuary and listened dazedly to President Mackay. What a startling sensation to realize all of a sudden that it was *our* son who had died, our little Ricky.

Miller Chapel, Princeton Theological Seminary

But reality and unreality seemed strangely intertwined, as a profusion of thoughts rushed wildly through my mind—mostly thoughts of Ricky, and of the miraculous events that had brought us to Princeton. Here I was, sitting in a chapel pew, about to begin my first semester as a seminary student. Not too many months before, I would have been the very last person to guess that I would ever leave the exciting world of professional baseball in order to enter the ministry.

But I knew as I sat in that Miller Chapel pew, even in the midst of my grief, that I was *called* to be there. I did not know *why* God had called me, but I never for a moment doubted *that* God had called me.

Now as I look back on my life, I can see how God's hand was at work in my life in remarkable ways. If I had to state very succinctly the motivational conviction of my life, it was and continues to be *the sense of being called*. To explain the basis of that conviction I need to back up a couple years prior to that convocation day.

Baltimore Bound—for Good?

On a cold, gray morning in late February 1955, Margie and I piled our suitcases, several boxes of work-related materials and files, and two of our three children into our old black Chevy and headed south. Our twenty-five-month-old son, Andy, was being left behind with his grandparents, to whom we had delivered him in Princeton the day before. His sister, Ellen, and brother, Ricky, who would celebrate their sixth and fifth birthdays, respectively, in March, were intrigued by the prospect of soon being able to go swimming in the Atlantic Ocean, while the friends they were leaving behind in Baltimore were still wearing snow boots and scarves.

We were bound for Miami, where the Baltimore Oriole pitchers and catchers were reporting for early spring training before moving north to Daytona Beach, where the full roster would report on March 1. One of the many enjoyable aspects of my work as public relations director of a major league baseball club was being in Florida for several weeks. Contrary to the false impression of some of my envious friends, this was an incredibly busy time for me, as I worked on all of the preseason publicity for the team, including the yearbook and the press guide; sent out press releases; dealt with the endless requests of visiting broadcasters, writers, and others; set up interviews, appeared on local radio and television stations; spoke at civic and service clubs; booked speaking engagements for other club officials and players; worked on promotional events; answered telephone calls and correspondence; and tried to keep up with what was going on in my office back in Baltimore. It certainly was no vacation.

But it was a delightful change of scenery and climate for me and my family, and in those days there was still an enchantment about being in sunny Florida, which was not nearly so crowded as it is now, while folks back home were battling snow-drifts and ice storms. The sound and sight of the waves breaking on the Atlantic shore, the palm trees swaying in the balmy ocean breeze, the colorfully casual dress of the part-time residents and tourists, the brilliant sunshine, the fluffy white clouds sailing the blue sky all added to the allure of the Floridian setting. The evenings cast a magic spell of their own, as even the plainest homes became bewitchingly lovely in the glow of the variegated floodlights that discreetly illuminated them.

Island Park, Daytona Beach, Florida, 1955. Spring-training home of the Baltimore Orioles. The Birds trained in Yuma, Arizona, the previous year.

For those of us connected with the ball club, the excitement of the experience was enhanced by the feeling of optimism that permeated the atmosphere of the spring training camp. Every team is a pennant contender in March, as the rookies vie for a place on the roster and the veterans set their sights on improving their stats from the previous season. Managers cautiously describe the scenarios for success, and publicity types like me paint rosy word pictures of the new personalities the fans will be watching in the coming months.

There was an added air of expectation in the Orioles' camp this year, under the leadership of their new manager/general manager Paul Richards, whose appointment had been announced by club president Clarence Miles on September 15. The tall Texan came to Baltimore from managing the Chicago White Sox to replace Jimmy Dykes and Arthur Ehlers, the previous manager and general manager respectively. Ehlers had given me my first front office job when he had been farm director of the erstwhile Philadelphia Athletics, and had been influential in my later being appointed the Athletics' first public relations director. I was personally pleased that Art was retained by the owners of the Orioles in another important administrative capacity. The affable Jimmy Dykes, with whom I had also worked when we were both with the Athletics, magnanimously agreed to finish out the season as manager.

Once Richards was on the scene, things had begun to happen. He had spent the off-season making player trades with other clubs and signing highly touted rookies to bonus contracts in a Herculean effort to improve the Orioles, who in 1954, their first American League season, had lost a hundred games and finished forty-six-and-a-half games behind the pennant-winning New York Yankees. His feverish negotiations climaxed on November 18 of that year when the Orioles and the

Orioles' manager Jimmy Dykes and White Sox manager Paul Richards with umpire Eddie Rommel prior to a game in 1954. Little did either manager know then that Richards would replace Dykes before the end of the season. The tall Texan would also replace Arthur Ehlers as general manager of the fledgling Orioles.

Yankees consummated the largest player trade between two major league clubs in baseball history. Seventeen players were involved in the mammoth exchange! I'll never forget how fast and furiously I had to bang away on my old Royal Standard typewriter to put out a detailed press release by the agreed-upon deadline—immediately! Despite that ambitious deal with the Yankees, the Orioles were destined for another losing season, this time finishing thirty-nine games out of first place, with only a slightly improved record of fifty-seven wins and ninety-seven losses.

But in Florida no one was anticipating a losing season. Quite to the contrary, there was talk of moving up to the first division, and some optimistic dreamers dared to hope the Orioles could even be in the thick of the pennant race, with the Wizard of Waxahachie at the helm. The Baltimore owners would need more than the genius of their brilliant strategist, however, to reverse the fortunes of the team they had inherited when they purchased the franchise of the inept St. Louis Browns in the fall of 1953. Richards knew he had accepted a huge challenge, but he proved himself equal to the task, as he laid the foundation for an Oriole dynasty that would become the winningest team in the majors for the next three decades.

The soft-spoken but often-outspoken Oriole manager was constantly hounded and surrounded by members of the press eager to gobble up his clever rejoinders and sometimes biting witticisms. He was, as they say in the trade, "good copy," and he obviously enjoyed his role as a managerial pundit, delivering his Delphic oracles to what soon became his coterie of admirers. One never knew when Paul would let slip something really newsworthy, such as a strategic decision to shift a player to a different position or his speculation about the opening-day starting pitcher or his frank assessment of a rookie's chances to make the squad. Every dugout or locker-room conversation was thus a potential news conference.

This reality was something I had to learn to live with. In the beginning it was a problem for me as the publicity person, who needed to know what was going on and what to say to the press when they looked to me for answers or for verification or clarification of something they had heard. I had to know what was on Richards's mind and have his complete confidence in order to be an effective spokesperson and interpreter to the press and to the club's other publics. I knew that degree of confidence would take time to build, since my new boss had, in a sense, inherited me. We had been working together during the fall and winter, when all the trading was going on, and he was comfortable with my handling of the numerous press releases and press conferences back in Baltimore.

Newly appointed Orioles' general manager Paul Richards holds his first press conference. He always gave the reporters much to write about.

4

My boyhood friend and former Princeton University baseball team-mate, Jack Dunn III, from whom the International League Orioles had been purchased by the new owners, and part of whose compensation included his being retained in a permanent executive position with the new organization, was then the traveling secretary for the team. Those familiar with professional baseball will know that this is an important and highly visible role in a major league club. The front office staff was much smaller in those days, and consequently the traveling secretary not only handled all the travel arrangements when the team was away but also functioned on the road as the liaison with the writers and broadcasters, since my public relations and promotional duties at home limited my traveling with the team. None of my P. R. counterparts traveled regularly with their teams. Most of us would usually make the circuit at least once a season to keep in touch with one another's activities, but the rest of the time we relied on the publicity departments of the host teams to serve the press when our own club was on the road.

Jack Dunn and I worked well together and enjoyed a close personal relationship. Jack was a proven baseball man, having played and managed professionally, as well as having owned and operated the International League Orioles. What especially endeared him to Paul Richards was the fact that Jack was also an excellent golfer, and Paul was an inveterate linksman, who found time to play often in Florida. Jack soon won Richards's total confidence and was constantly in his company. He became a regular member of the private audience who would sit in Paul's office swapping jokes and stories and listening to the Great Man pontificate. I excluded myself by choice from those gatherings, not because I would not have enjoyed being there, but because there were too many more-urgent things I had to do.

Jack Dunn, former owner of the International League Orioles, became vice president of the new American League Orioles, serving first as traveling secretary and later as assistant general manager.

Consequently, I was always somewhat worried that I might be missing something. It wasn't that Paul Richards was intentionally uncooperative. It was a case of "out of sight is out of mind." I checked in with him a couple times a day to see if he had any news, or if there was anything I needed to know, but that was not the most reliable way to learn what was on his mind. Jack Dunn was most helpful in reporting things he had picked up from Paul in the office chitchats or on the golf course, and in reminding Paul to bring me into the process whenever he had an official announcement to make.

Paul could see I was busy, and I had the definite feeling that he appreciated what I was doing, and respected what I stood for. He was always most cordial and friendly, but to conform to his operating style would have compromised my own work ethic, and I simply could not waste that kind of time. Shortly before we moved up to Daytona Beach to begin the regular spring training with the full roster of players, I caught Paul alone in his office at the stadium and shared my honest feelings on the whole matter. "I don't like to miss anything, Paul, but I have so much to do; I just don't have time to sit around and shoot the breeze."

When I had finished telling him some of the things I was trying to do, he smiled and said, "I understand, Dick. Think nothing of it. I'll let you know if anything important comes up."

From that point on I felt much more relaxed about our relationship, and much less concerned about not being one of his golf-playing buddies. *Patsies* would be a better term in my case, since I would have joined the long line of his victims on the golf course. In all my years of spring training with the Athletics and the Orioles I rarely could find time to play golf, although I enjoyed the game immensely.

Meanwhile, Jack Dunn would complain to me privately about how much precious time he was having to spend with Paul. "Why do you have to play golf with him, Jack?" I asked very pointedly. "Can't you tell him you have other things to do?"

"Yes, but I'm afraid he would stop asking me," my friend replied with a grin. He had a point.

That was the beginning of a series of conversations that Jack and I had about personal integrity and the ethics of compromise. Both of us were concerned about the lavish style of the new manager/general manager and his extravagant and often wasteful spending of the club's money, whether for bonus players who amounted to nothing, or for his own personal expenses. It was more reckless than dishonest, but it bothered both of us.

Having been used to the necessary frugality of the Philadelphia Athletics, and the conscientious stewardship of Paul's predecessor, Art Ehlers, I was disturbed by the drastic change in operating styles.

At the same time, both Jack and I needed to be in the good graces of the man whose actions and decisions impacted our lives in different ways. Undoubtedly our different approaches to the problem reflected our perspectives on our future careers. Jack needed Paul's friendship and confidence to cement the advisory role he was developing with the new "m/gm." He was willing to accept Paul's operating style and to overlook his extravagant spending on the grounds that it was not his place to question it, nor did it keep Jack from doing his job.

I agreed with Jack at the time, that it was not our place to question Paul's spending habits. He was the boss and accountable to the board of directors, not to us. My personal problem was whether I wanted to work for a man who operated the way he did. More to the point, could I do my job well, given the relationship I had defined? The much larger and more important question was whether I wanted to remain in baseball or to explore some other attractive possibilities that were presenting themselves.

I had left the Athletics to begin a new career as the copy-and-plans director of the W. Wallace Orr Advertising Agency in Philadelphia. My ties with baseball had not been entirely severed, for our agency was immediately engaged to handle the advertising and to produce the promotional materials for the Athletics. Thus I was doing some of the same work I had been doing, while wearing a different hat. When the Boston Braves moved to Milwaukee, we were also given a rush order to design and produce the ticket brochures and other materials for the Milwaukee Braves' first season.

I had been with the agency only a year when my advertising career was abruptly ended by a turn of events that was not altogether unexpected. On October 26, 1953, it was announced that the St. Louis Browns franchise had been purchased by a group of civic-minded Marylanders headed by Clarence Miles, a Baltimore/Washington attorney. The Browns would cease to be, and the new American League Orioles would replace Baltimore's triple-A, International League franchise. That was the end of the highly successful Dunn dynasty, which had owned and operated the triple-A Baltimore Orioles for three generations. In 1944 the minor league Orioles had exceeded the home attendance of ten major league clubs, and during the Little World Series with Louisville that year had drawn a minor league record crowd one night of 52,833! Baltimore had impressively proved itself to be an outstanding sports town, and many had long believed the city was destined one day to return to the major leagues.

That day had finally come! My former boss, Arthur Ehlers, had been named general manager of the new organization. The announcement evoked within me the strong feeling that I would be offered the public relations job with the new Orioles. Margie and I spent another late night discussing this possibility. It was indeed exciting to think about returning to my hometown to help launch the major league Orioles. We were not at all sure, however, that we wanted to return to the baseball "rat race" so soon after my having begun a new career that seemed to offer unlimited possibilities down the road. We had become accustomed, furthermore, to our less-pressurized existence, and I was enjoying being able to spend more nights and weekends at home with Margie and the children. She had been a "baseball widow" long enough, with my being gone for so many night games during the season and my gallivanting around the banquet circuit during the off-season.

Philadelphia Athletics president Connie Mack, on his team's first visit to Memorial Stadium, is flanked by Orioles vice president Jim Keelty (L) and Arthur Ehlers (R), in an unfinished visitors' box in the still-under-construction stadium.

We finally decided that if the Orioles should approach me, I would make the price of my accepting the position high enough that if they met my terms, I could not refuse.

Sure enough, the next night I received a telephone call from Art Ehlers. His tone of voice was that of a person with good news to impart. Art reported that he had recommended me to head the public relations department and asked if I would be interested in the job. My presentiment of his call did not diminish the excitement that my voice in turn must have conveyed. I asked Art if I could come to his house and discuss it with him in person. "Come on over," he said.

It took me only a few minutes to drive the short distance from our house to the Ehlers' home, where Margie and I had had many a delightful meal. Art greeted me with a smile almost as broad as his huge frame: "I want you to come with me to Baltimore!"

I thanked my friend profusely and assured him I was excited and flattered by his recommendation. "I must tell you that I had a feeling I might hear from you. Margie and I had a long discussion last night about what we would do if the Orioles should offer me a job. It would be fun, of course, to be involved in setting up a new ball club and helping to promote major league baseball in my own hometown. But at this point we both have some reservations about my quitting what I'm now doing." I described my varied involvements at the agency and what I liked about the work. "It would be hard to leave all that, Art. I guess it depends on the salary."

"What would it take for you to say yes?"

Without hesitation I named the figure Margie and I had decided upon. It was considerably higher than my current salary at the agency and twice as much as I had been making with the Athletics.

"I'll be talking with Clarence Miles tomorrow. Why don't you stop by again tomorrow night? I'll have the answer for you then."

Our discussion continued for another hour or more, and I felt my excitement mounting as Art shared his plans and visions for the Orioles. When I returned home, Margie was anxiously waiting for my report of the conversation, the implications of which were beginning to sink in. What if they met my terms? We would be moving to Baltimore. What would I say to my boss, Wally Orr? Neither one of us slept well that night.

The next evening I dropped by Art's house as planned. His first words as he opened the door said it all: "Welcome aboard!" He told me Clarence Miles had accepted my terms without hesitation and wanted me to start to work as soon as possible. "He's looking forward to meeting you." Art's glowing elaboration of Mr. Miles's enthusiasm caused me momentarily to wonder if I should not have set the terms even higher!

"I want you to come with me to Baltimore!" My first boss with the Philadelphia Athletics was farm director Arthur Ehlers, who later became general manager of the A's. He was also responsible for my being hired by the Orioles, when he was named general manager of the newly formed Baltimore baseball club. With the appointment of Paul Richards as general manager, Art Ehlers was shifted to another administrative post in the Orioles' organization.

9

The moment of decision had arrived. I grasped Art's extended hand. "Okay, I guess that means we move to Baltimore! It will be great to be working with you again, Art—especially since we'll both be going back to our hometown."

Art said Mr. Miles would announce my appointment the following Monday, November 2, in the Baltimore papers. We visited for a couple more hours talking about all the things that needed to be done in connection with bringing major league baseball back to Baltimore. Unlike during our discussion the night before, I was now speaking with the animation of one who would be involved in that thrilling enterprise.

Margie was understandably less enthusiastic when I told her the news. She was well aware of the implications of my return to baseball. But she was happy for me and shared my excitement at the prospect of helping to launch a major league baseball club in my hometown.

One of our immediate concerns was having to tender my resignation to the president of the advertising agency, W. Wallace Orr. I wanted to tell him in person before he read it in the newspapers. Knowing that he was terribly busy trying to meet a production deadline, I nevertheless telephoned him on Sunday evening, November 1, at the studio of our subsidiary, Tel Ra Productions, a pioneer in sports television programming. "I need to see you, Wally," I said. "May I come down to the studio?"

"What about?" he asked.

"I'll tell you when I see you," I replied.

"Okay. Come on down."

Driving downtown that night from our home on Linden Drive in Merwood Park, a suburban section north of Philadelphia's City Line Avenue, took about forty minutes, during which time I rehearsed different ways of telling Wally the news. He had been so kind and supportive during the short time I had been with him that I dreaded what his reaction would be to the announcement that I was going back into baseball. By the time I entered the studio, I had finally figured out what to say.

Wally walked over to me as soon as he saw me, and before I had uttered a word, he said, "I think you ought to take it!"

"How did you know?" I asked, caught completely by surprise.

"As soon as Baltimore got the franchise, I figured they'd come after you," he replied. "But tell me about it."

I told Wally that Art Ehlers had recommended me to the new owners, and that they had made me an offer I could not refuse. I confided in Wally

10

that one reason for some hesitancy on my part was that my father, who had been the business manager of the International League Orioles, had been retained, along with Jack Dunn, in their same respective capacities with the major league club. I respected my father more than any other man I have ever known, and I loved him dearly. From my boyhood up we had always been the best of friends. It was not that I worried about our working in the same organization, but that I wondered whether people would assume that he had been responsible for my getting the job, and whether or not I could be my own person and not just Herb Armstrong's son. After talking it over, my dad and I had agreed that there was nothing to worry about. We would be coming to the new Orioles through different doors, and we both felt people would understand that.

Wally was genuinely happy for me. "I hate to lose you, Dick, but it's a wonderful opportunity for you. And it's your hometown. When do you need to go?"

"As soon as possible," I replied. "I'll leave everything in order, and we can keep in touch, if you need me for any reason."[1]

The next day, November 2, the announcement of my appointment appeared in the Philadelphia newspapers, having been picked up by the wire services. That precipitated a barrage of telephone calls from friends and well-wishers. Two days later I took a train to Washington, DC, to meet with President Clarence Miles in his law office. I liked this refined gentleman from the very start. He understood that I was uncertain at that point in my life about pursuing a long-term career in baseball, but we agreed to a two-year commitment on my part and an open-ended contract after that.

On the morning of November 15 Margie drove me and several bulging suitcases to the North Philadelphia train station, and I was off to Baltimore. The next day I moved into my temporary office on Eager Street near the center of downtown Baltimore to begin my part of the huge task of preparing for the inaugural season of the new American League Orioles. Construction on the stadium that was to be the home of the Orioles and the professional football Baltimore Colts was proceeding apace. The front office was working feverishly, and for me it meant sixteen and sometimes eighteen hours a day on the job.

---

1. Neither Wally nor I could ever have dreamed then that I would ever be a minister, let alone the one who would conduct his funeral service several years later (June 7, 1962).

2440 Linden Drive, our home in Merwood Park, just outside of Philadelphia.

Meanwhile, Margie was back in Merwood Park, Pennsylvania, with the twenty-four-hour-a-day task of caring for our three young children and trying to keep our little Dutch colonial house ready for inspection by potential buyers. She always sounded cheerful during our nightly telephone conversations, but on my too-infrequent visits home, I could see how difficult it was for her to have to manage everything with very little help from me. Even when all three children were sick with the chicken pox at the same time, she never complained, knowing the kind of pressure I was under in Baltimore. I was boarding temporarily with my folks, while scouting for a new home, the purchase of which was contingent upon the sale of our home in Havertown.

Months went by without so much as a nibble. The real estate market in our area was distressingly soft. In February, when it was time for spring training, the house still had not been sold. Margie and I were tired of living apart. She and the children drove with me to Yuma, Arizona, where the Orioles trained for the 1954 season. We treasured our time together in the car on the way out and back. We hoped our real estate agent would have good news for us when we returned, but it was not to be. By the time the season opened, we still hadn't been able to move.

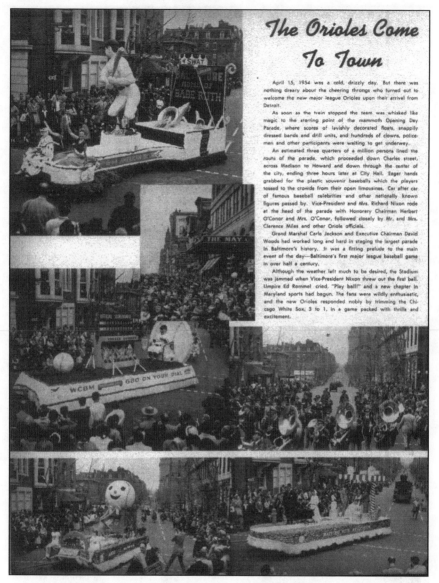

The Orioles Come To Town

April 15, 1954 was a cold, drizzly day. But there was nothing dreary about the cheering throngs who turned out to welcome the new major league Orioles upon their arrival from Detroit.

As soon as the train stopped the team was whisked like magic to the starting point of the mammoth Opening Day Parade, where scores of lavishly decorated floats, snappily dressed bands and drill units, and hundreds of clowns, policemen and other participants were waiting to get underway.

An estimated three quarters of a million persons lined the route of the parade, which proceeded down Charles street, across Madison to Howard and down through the center of the city, ending three hours later at City Hall. Eager hands grabbed for the plastic souvenir baseballs which the players tossed to the crowds from their open limousines. Car after car of famous baseball celebrities and other nationally known figures passed by. Vice-President and Mrs. Richard Nixon rode at the head of the parade with Honorary Chairman Herbert O'Conor and Mrs. O'Conor, followed closely by Mr. and Mrs. Clarence Miles and other Oriole officials.

Grand Marshal Carle Jackson and Executive Chairman David Woods had worked long and hard in staging the largest parade in Baltimore's history. It was a fitting prelude to the main event of the day—Baltimore's first major league baseball game in over half a century.

Although the weather left much to be desired, the Stadium was jammed when Vice-President Nixon threw out the first ball. Umpire Ed Rommel cried, "Play ball!" and a new chapter in Maryland sports had begun. The fans were wildly enthusiastic, and the new Orioles responded nobly by trimming the Chicago White Sox, 3 to 1, in a game packed with thrills and excitement.

A page from the 1955 Oriole Yearbook. The opening-day parade was an auspicious introduction to a miserable maiden season for the Orioles.

The Orioles' debut was auspicious. On April 15, 1954, several hundred thousand people lined the streets for the huge opening-day parade, the largest in Baltimore's history, to greet the newly arrived team. The Birds responded by defeating the Washington Senators that afternoon 3 to 1, behind the stellar pitching of "Bullet Bob" Turley. For the rest of the season, however, it was pretty much downhill. Despite their dismal showing on the field that first year, the Orioles drew over a million fans, who were thrilled just to be watching major league baseball in Baltimore's beautiful new Memorial Stadium. Ironically, the baseball one-day attendance record for Memorial Stadium was set not by the major league Orioles but by the International League club.

Top: May 16, 1954. Memorial Stadium was packed for the Sunday afternoon doubleheader between the Orioles and the Yankees. Don Larsen went the distance for the Birds in the second game to garner his first win of the season, holding the Yankees to three hits in a well-pitched 6–2 victory. Maybe the New York powers-that-be recalled that victory when they later acquired Larsen in a seventeen-player off-season trade. Win or lose, the Baltimore fans were excited to be watching major league baseball in their new stadium. *Bottom*: Aerial view of Memorial Stadium. Baltimore City College, the third-oldest boys' public high school in the United States, is in the upper-left corner, and Eastern High School for girls is in the center just above the stadium. The Orioles moved to their new home at Camden Yards in 1992, and Memorial Stadium eventually became the second of my former baseball workplaces to be demolished, Connie Mack Stadium having been razed in 1976.

Top: This is old Oriole Park on 29th Street, home of the International League Orioles until it was destroyed by fire on July 4, 1944. I remember the date well, because I was home on leave from the Navy and pitched batting practice for the Orioles that night. The Orioles outdrew ten of the major league teams that year, a feat that paved the way for Baltimore eventually to become a major league franchise. *Middle*: Baltimore Stadium, October 10, 1944. On this night, playing under the lights of the reconfigured football stadium, the International League champion Orioles defeated the American Association pennant winners, the Louisville Colonels, 10–0 before 52,833 fans, the largest crowd in minor league history and the largest ever to see a baseball game in Maryland before or since. The Orioles won the 1944 Junior World Series four games to two and outdrew ten of the major league clubs that year. *Bottom*: On the exterior wall of Memorial Stadium, behind home plate, was a huge dedicatory inscription to the veterans of World Wars I and II. A small replica of the wall has been erected outside Oriole Park at Camden Yards.

That was not good enough for the new owners, however, who were not used to the kind of public criticism a losing team arouses, even when the preseason expectations had been justifiably low. Unaccustomed to living in the limelight of professional sports, these well-meaning businessmen overreacted to the often-critical articles of the sportswriters and the negative comments of fans. Needing a scapegoat, they settled on the general manager and manager, and summarily fired Arthur Ehlers and Jimmy Dykes. Although I was Ehlers's protégé, I was fortunate enough to escape the purge. My father, whose reputation and long-standing leadership in the sports world were un-matched in the state of Maryland, was also retained as business manager.

For me personally the glamour of professional sports and the sheer fun of working for a ball club overshadowed the losing season, which was dis-appointing but not unexpected given the disastrous record of the St. Louis Browns the year before. I had not realized how much I missed baseball while I had been in advertising, and it felt great to be back in the game again.

There was, nevertheless, a lingering feeling of uncertainty about the direction I wanted my life to take. The brief venture into advertising and into radio and television production had whetted my appetite for other cre-ative ventures, including one which seemed at the time to have unlimited financial possibilities. Some friends and I had produced some jingles (song ads) and were seriously considering expanding that profitable sideline into a full-time enterprise as an adjunct to the agency, with the encouragement of its president, Wally Orr. That possibility had been abruptly terminated, however, when I had accepted the position with the Orioles.

Now it was 1955, and here I was in Daytona Beach for the Orioles' second spring-training season. With the change in management, the ques-tion of occupations had resurfaced, and Margie and I talked long and hard about the various possibilities and options. I was leaning more and more toward a long-range career in baseball, with the aspiration of becoming a general manager one day. That was more than a remote possibility, for I had already been offered such a position with a triple-A club. I had declined in view of my interest in exploring other possibilities outside baseball. At the time I had felt that my present position with a major league club was a more advantageous springboard. Personal ambition had admittedly been a primary motivation in that decision.

It was not the determinative factor, however, in the internal wrestling match in which I was intensely engaged. Now it was more a matter of per-sonal fulfillment, complicated by a question of professional ethics. I had an opportunity to verbalize my dilemma one evening when Margie and I were visiting in our Daytona Plaza motel suite with Jack and Mary Rose Dunn and Ernie and Lulu Harwell. Ernie, who is now better remembered as the highly respected, longtime play-by-play announcer of the Detroit Tigers, was then the number-one radio and television announcer for the Orioles.

We had become close friends. During a philosophical discussion, as we were theorizing about the ethics of compromise, Ernie, a very percep-tive person, had asked how we were getting along with the new "m/gm."

Jack and I tried tactfully to describe our respective predicaments, knowing Ernie to be a man of the highest discretion and tact. Ernie's succinct advice to me was, "Do it your way!" At the end of that evening I was more convinced than ever that I could be my own man and still function effectively in my role as public relations director.

I continued the discussion with Margie later that night. The next morning I awakened with a clear and strong conviction that I belonged in baseball and nowhere else. Where could I find a more enjoyable career, and one that offered so many psychic income factors? I felt a new excitement about my job and a refreshing peace of mind about my future. For the first time, really, I was certain about where I was going and what I wanted to do with my life. It was as if a heavy weight had been lifted from my shoulders.

Margie was as pleased as I about this turn of affairs, for she had had to live with my vacillating career ambitions. I wondered why I had been tempted to consider any other occupation, when baseball had always been my first love and offered such a promising future. Whatever hidden feeling of temporariness I had brought with me to Baltimore was completely and, I was sure, permanently gone.

In my state of euphoria never could I have imagined that something was about to happen that would change my life completely.

Orioles broadcaster Ernie Harwell emcees on Joe Coleman Day, as president Clarence Miles presents a check to the veteran Baltimore hurler.

2

God Had Other Plans

I was, to borrow a phrase from a Broadway musical of that era, "the most happy fella"!

But I was no less busy. I loved my work, and, believe it or not, I loved being busy. I actually thrived under pressure; and the more things I had going on at once, the better I liked it. In what seemed no time at all, the so-called Grapefruit League had begun. That's when the teams that are training in Florida play exhibition games against one another. The crescendo of excitement and activity accelerates, and there is even less time to relax.

Spring training was always a hectic time for me, and Ricky and Ellen were happy whenever their Daddy could spend time with them. Here we are in West Palm Beach, Florida, spring training home of the Philadelphia Athletics, in March 1952.

The one negative aspect of my having to go at such a furious pace was that I saw very little of Margie and the children throughout the week. It was no different during the regular season. In fact, my lack of availability to the family was one of the reasons I had left baseball to join an advertising agency, where I thought I could maintain a more normal working schedule. During spring training my best time with the children was in the morning before I left for the ballpark, and in the early evening, before Margie and I would head out to dinner at a local restaurant with whomever we were entertaining that night. Occasionally I was able to slip back to the motel to spend an hour or two with the children, and we would have our own ball games on the spacious front lawn of the Daytona Plaza. Margie and I were together for dinner every night but almost never alone.

One evening we decided we needed a break, so we engaged our regular babysitter for the evening and drove to Johnston's Coffee Shop, our favorite restaurant, for another delicious, and this time, relaxing meal. Although we enjoyed the company of visiting writers and radio and TV personalities, when we were entertaining I was still on the job, and that put a certain pressure on both Margie and me. So it was wonderful to be by ourselves this one night, as we had so much to talk about and so many things to share. By the time Margie had filled me in on all the things she and the children had been doing, and I had reported on my activities, it was time to head back to the motel, as we had promised to have our babysitter home at a reasonable hour.

It was still twilight as we were driving north on the Dixie Highway, but most of the cars had their headlights on by now. Margie and I were calmly chatting, when—without warning—something strange and wonderful happened. *I was suddenly seized by an overpowering feeling that God was speaking to me!*

So irresistible was the sensation that I immediately pulled over on the wide shoulder of the road and stopped the car. I sat there tensely gripping the wheel, with what must have been a stunned expression on my face, staring at nothing. Margie was startled. She was afraid I was having a heart attack. "Are you all right?" she asked, worriedly.

For a moment I was unable to speak. Then I turned toward her and said in a tone that reflected my bewilderment, "I have the strangest feeling that God is telling me that I must become a minister!"

I heard no audible voice. I saw no vision of God. There was no blinding light or ghostly glow. But I felt the presence of God, and it was awesome, even terrifying. Never had I experienced anything like it, nor had I any words to describe it.

Margie listened quietly, as I tried to verbalize what I was feeling. She was not experiencing what I was experiencing, but she knew something miraculous had happened to me. As always, in her beautifully sensitive way she knew that then was not the time to speak. Her caring expression communicated her love and concern as she watched me struggling with my thoughts. We sat there in silence while I tried to understand what had happened.

After a few minutes, I turned on the ignition, and as we pulled out on to the highway, I said, "We have to talk about this. I can't understand what has happened to me, but it's very real, and it's kind of scary. It's as if an inner voice is telling me that I have to become a minister, and I don't know what that means."

I knew that I had been in the presence of God, and I knew God wanted me to become a minister, but I didn't know what I was supposed to do about it.

After I returned from taking the babysitter home, Margie and I sat up most of the night discussing the implications of what had happened. Neither one of us could understand why and how this could happen to me only a few days after I had decided so enthusiastically and definitely to make professional baseball my permanent career. Ever since my college days I had been considering various options, and my decisions had always been based on considerations of money and prestige. Throughout my years in baseball and advertising I had toyed with many interesting ideas, but never had I had the slightest inkling about being a minister, nor had anyone ever suggested the ministry to me. It was not a matter of ruling out the possibility; the thought had never occurred to me.

That being the case, what had happened to me in the car that night was all the more incredible. The more Margie and I talked about it, the more certain I became that I had no choice in the matter. This was not just an idle notion that had crossed my mind, or a new possibility that had just occurred to me, as others had in the past. Nor was it even some kind of compulsive urge that had come over me unexpectedly. Rather it was an all-consuming conviction in response to the unmistakable presence and irresistible will of God, which had been revealed to me in an intimate and traumatic way.

Margie was wonderfully wise as she helped me sort out the questions that needed to be addressed, but it quickly became clear to both of us that I needed to talk to someone who could provide some answers. We agreed that I should see a minister the next morning.

But where was I to find one? In all our years of going to Florida, not once had we ever been to church. Sunday like every other day was a working day for me. But I remembered having driven past a large church not too far from our hotel on my way to the ballpark. So, early the next morning I pulled into the church parking lot. The sign on the church lawn suggested it was the right place for someone like me, for it read: "The Tourist Church."

Yet it was with some trepidation that I walked up to the door leading to the church office. I was afraid it might be too early, but the door was unlocked, and I walked in. I found myself in a wide hallway with lots of doors, all of which were closed, and there was not a soul in sight. Then I heard footsteps and a friendly-looking middle-aged man came round the corner at the end of the corridor.

"Excuse me, sir," I said, "would you happen to know if the minister is in?"

He smiled and replied, "He is indeed! My name is Dr. Gordon Poteat. I'm the pastor here. What can I do for you?"

His amiable manner put me more at ease. "Would you have a few minutes to talk? I need some advice, and I didn't know where to turn."

"Of course. Come into my study, where we can be more comfortable. No one else is here at the moment."

It was still early, and other members of the staff had not yet arrived. It just so happened that Dr. Poteat had come in early that morning and had appeared in the hallway just as I entered the building. A few seconds later he would have been in his study, and I would not have known he was in the building. That was the first of many occasions in the days following when I would found myself thinking or saying, "it just so happened that . . ." The word *providential* was not yet part of my vocabulary.

"How can I help you?" Dr. Poteat asked as he seated me in a comfortable easy chair in his spacious and well-appointed study. I remember being impressed by the paneled walls, the floor-to-ceiling shelves of books, and the orderliness of his huge desk. Apart from the time Margie and I had met with her pastor prior to our wedding, I had not sought help from a pastor since my days in the Navy, when I had had some intimate discussions with the chaplain aboard the *USS Chandeleur* (AV10).

The U.S.S. Chandeleur (AV10), on which I served as Disbursing Officer and later as Supply Officer. We were the first ship to be put into "moth balls" in the 16th Fleet, and as Supply Officer I had the responsibility of supervising the decommissioning process.

I had thought of him more as a friend than as a counselor, but in retrospect I came to realize that Chaplain Elmer Kimmell, a Methodist minister, had played an important part in preparing me for what was now happening.

Being unfamiliar, therefore, with the principle of pastoral confidentiality, I felt it necessary to obtain Dr. Poteat's guarantee that what we were about to discuss would never get outside the walls of that room. After apologizing for my unannounced appearance and thanking him for his willingness to see me on the spur of the moment, I plunged right in. "My name is Dick Armstrong. I happen to be the public relations director of the Baltimore Orioles . . ."

"Is that so?" Dr. Poteat appeared dutifully impressed, not as if I were a celebrity, but because I was with the Orioles, for it just so happened (!) that he was a baseball fan.

"If anyone were to find out about what I'm going to tell you," I continued, "it would be very embarrassing to me, so I hope you won't breathe a word of this to anyone."

Dr. Poteat smiled. "Of course not!" he said, showing no annoyance, but in a tone that indicated the inappropriateness of my concern.

"You understand," I went on to apologize as much as to explain, "when you're in baseball, you're in the public limelight, and if this ever got out it would be all over the papers. I'm not ready for that. I don't even understand it myself."

"Tell me what happened." He was looking at me more intently now, but still with a kind expression that made it easy for me to continue.

"I've had a strange experience and I need to talk to a minister who understands these things. Last night as my wife, Margie, and I were driving back to the Daytona Plaza from the restaurant where we had eaten, something amazing happened. I suddenly felt as if God was speaking to me, right there in the car! Nothing like that has ever happened to me before. I have to say it was really frightening! I didn't see anything or hear a voice or anything like that, but there was this weird feeling that God was telling me that I have to become a minister! Do things like that happen to people? Could that really have been God? Or was it just my imagination?—But I know it was God!"

"Yes, things like that can happen to people, and do happen. God can be very real and very present at times. And God calls people in many different ways. It doesn't happen that way to most people, and it didn't happen that way to me, but it certainly can happen."

"But why would God want me to become a minister? I'm the most unlikely candidate he could pick." There was no false modesty in that statement. I was being totally honest and sincere, for I could not even imagine myself as a minister.

"What makes you say that?" Dr. Poteat asked.

"Because I'm not what you would call a religious person. Oh, I've always believed in God, and I attend different churches whenever I can, but I've never been active in a church. As a boy I never attended Sunday school, and I've never read the Bible. And besides all that, I have other things I want to do with my life." I told Dr. Poteat how I had come to my recent decision to make baseball my permanent career, and how good I had felt about that intention. "Is it possible that God would call someone like me?"

"Of course! God calls all sorts of people from all walks of life."

"But I know nothing about the Bible or about the church or about being a minister, and very little about Christianity in general."

"That's what seminaries are for!"

The mention of the word *seminary* instantly conjured up thoughts of black-robed, somber-faced, monkish individuals strolling silently through barren halls with their hands folded. "You mean I'd have to go to seminary? How long would that take?"

"Ordinarily it takes three years to get your basic theological degree."

"Three years! How in the world can I do that? That would mean resigning from the Orioles. I'm married and have three children. I just can't stop working and go to school for three years. We have very little money in the bank. You see, our five-year-old son has had leukemia for about a year. Most of our savings have been used to meet his medical needs. How would I support my family while I am attending seminary? How would we survive?"

"I'm sorry to hear about your son. In view of your situation, you may well qualify for financial aid, or for a work-study loan. You can explain your need when you apply to a seminary."

"I don't know where to begin. How do I choose a seminary? Do you have any to recommend? To whom should I write?"

"That depends." Dr. Poteat thought for a moment and then asked, "Are you a denominationalist?"

Not having heard that term before, I replied, "No, I'm an Episcopalian." I assumed that being a denominationalist was like being an Episcopalian or a Methodist.

My answer to his question brought forth another smile from my counselor. "That's what I mean," said Dr. Poteat. "In other words, you do have a denominational affiliation, but you apparently haven't been active. Probably you would be most comfortable in a nondenominational seminary." He gave me the names of four seminaries, three of which were Baptist institutions. Dr. Poteat, it turned out, was a Baptist minister, although one could not have known that from the name of his church. Now that I know the difference between a congregational (autonomous) and a denominational (connectional) polity, I understand his use of the word *denominationalist*, which for a Baptist makes a legitimate distinction.

Dr. Poteat continued, "I suggest you address your letter to the director of admissions in each case and simply state that you feel called into the ministry, that you are exploring the possibility of quitting your job in order to enter seminary, and that you are inquiring if there would be any financial aid available."

Dr. Poteat and I chatted for several more minutes, during which time I asked him if by any chance he knew the Rev. Vernon Richardson, the very popular pastor of the University Baptist Church on Charles Street, opposite the main entrance to the campus of Johns Hopkins University. "I certainly do!" replied Dr. Poteat. "Vernon was one of my prize students at Crozier Theological Seminary when I was on the faculty there."

"Isn't that amazing! University Church is just a few blocks away from my parents' home. When I was living with them, I worshiped there more than anywhere else, because I enjoyed Dr. Richardson's preaching. He's one of the best speakers I've ever heard."

When I stood up to leave, Dr. Poteat reassured me that I had experienced a genuine call of God and urged me to trust that God would open the way for me to go to seminary. As he escorted me out the door, he asked about the Orioles' chances for the coming season, and I invited him to attend one of the spring-training games as my guest. He was quick to accept my offer. "Does that invitation include my wife?" he asked with a grin.

"By all means! Just tell me which day you'd like to attend and I'll leave two tickets for you at the reserved-seat window."

I could hardly contain my excitement as I ran out to the parking lot and jumped into my car. Instead of continuing on to the ballpark, I drove back to the motel, where Margie was eagerly waiting to hear what had happened. I gave her almost a word-for-word account of my conversation with

Dr. Poteat, the bottom line result of which was the first confirmation of my call into the ministry.

I was not thinking of it in these terms then, but now I look upon that conversation as the first of many doors God opened along my path to seminary. What if the pastor's response to my story had been overly cautious or skeptical or even totally negative? What effect would that have had on me as I tried to understand a profoundly religious experience? I'll never know. The point is that God had opened the first door by leading me to just the right person, who gave me the initial encouragement I needed.

From that fateful night on, Margie and I could talk about little else whenever we were alone. We realized that we could not discuss our secret with anyone at that time, not even with our parents. There were too many bridges to cross, too many obstacles to be overcome before we would dare announce my intention to resign from the Orioles in order to enter the ministry. I knew it was something I had to do, but I had no idea how or when.

I also have to confess to being a bit embarrassed about what had happened to me. I dreaded the thought of being teased about it. I could imagine the players calling me "Deacon Dick," and the owners wondering if my heart was still in my work, and hundreds of eager beavers wanting my job. There were also fears relating to the practical problem of supporting myself and my family while attending seminary. And what impact would such a move have on our children, especially Ricky?

Despite these fears, the call of God became clearer and stronger every day, as Margie and I continued to reflect on the Dixie Highway experience and its implications for our lives. We were praying for God's guidance, and our prayers were answered in surprising ways. For instance, we began to see a connection between some rather remarkable happenings and what I now refer to as my Damascus Road experience.

3

The Journey Begins

As a biblically illiterate Episcopalian, I didn't know enough about the New Testament to speak of what had happened to me as a Damascus Road experience. Nor was I theologically mature enough to understand how God provides for those whom God calls.

Two days after that unforgettable night a letter arrived in the mail addressed to our son Ricky in care of us. It was from one of my very closest boyhood friends and schoolmates back in Baltimore. The gist of the handwritten note was as follows:

> *Dear Ricky, for a long time I've been wanting to do something for you and your parents, but I know they are proud and do not want to accept help from any of their friends. So I'm enclosing this check, not for them but for you. I want them to use it in whatever way is best for you. They can't refuse it, because it's for you. It comes with all of my love and best wishes.*
>
> *Wilson Ballard*

Margie and I were deeply touched not only by Wilson's generous gift but by the sensitive manner in which he gave it. It just so happened that it came at a time when we were worrying about our finances, but we didn't at first see the connection between that unexpected gift and my call to ministry. Never in my life, except at Christmas or on my birthday, had anyone other than my family ever given me money. But out of the blue came this gracious gift from a caring friend.

With the hindsight of faith I came to see that it was God's way of saying, "Don't worry. I will provide." But I did not understand that at first. I had so much to learn!

A few days later there came another letter in the mail, this one addressed to Margie and me. It was from the Suburban Squires, a group of gentlemen songsters I had sung with in our Philadelphia days. They had made a record and had decided to give the bulk of the proceeds to us! "What better way," they had asked themselves, "can we use this money than to help two of our friends whose little boy needs it much more than we do?" Enclosed with their beautifully worded letter was a sizeable check! But I was still slow to make the connection!

Top Left: Rehearsing with the Suburban Squires, under the direction of Princeton classmate and fellow Nassoon Jim Buck (seated at the piano). Jim later became one of the owners of the Philadelphia Phillies. *Top Right*: Close harmony! Ed Emack, who became a very close friend, is in the upper right corner. Ed has a powerful, deep bass voice—the kind every good barbershop quartet needs. *Bottom Left*: November 1946. The reconstituted post-WWII Nassoons were making their first public appearance. They were performing on the stage of Princeton University's Alexander Hall. They are booked solidly through June. *Bottom Right*: Here Jim Buck (third from left) and I (second from right) are singing with the Princeton Nassoons in the 1946 Triangle Show, Clear the Track.

In the same week came yet another letter containing a check. It was from my good friend John Jackson, president of the Jay Publishing Company, who published the yearbooks of most of the major league clubs. John had called me a few days before we left for Florida to see if I'd be willing to do the player write-ups for the yearbooks of the Detroit Tigers and my former team, the Philadelphia Athletics. Neither organization had anyone to perform that chore. I wanted to help my friend, although it would mean my having to burn whatever midnight oil was left in my energy lamp.

Nothing had been said about money, and I had not expected to be paid; but a few days later I received a letter from John, confirming the arrangement and stating a figure he intended to pay me for my time and effort. It was fair compensation, unexpected on my part but very much appreciated. I had forgotten about being compensated until the check arrived in the mail. The fact that it arrived when it did seemed more than coincidental.

I was beginning to get the message! It was not that God was rewarding me for responding to the call. Nor was there any element of bargaining in my soul-searching. I had made no demands of God or set any conditions for doing what I knew God wanted me to do. In retrospect I view those three unlooked-for checks, coming in rapid succession in the space of a few days, as God's way of teaching me the meaning of providence. God provides for those whom God calls!

That statement is an affirmation of faith. The unbelieving world does not understand the truth of it. Unbelievers view the extraordinary nature and timing of an unsought boon or blessing as a fortuitous coincidence, a stroke of luck, mere chance. But to the eyes of faith it is the providence of God. Cynical agnostics and skeptical unbelievers reject such an affirmation as one's biased rationalization of past events to conform to one's presuppositions about God.

In a sense they are right, for God's providential care is not a provable fact, and I know that my belief in God and my statements about God are not self-evident to an unbeliever. One's experience of God is not a reason for someone else to believe, but it is the basis of one's own convictions. What happened to me on the Dixie Highway was a spiritual watershed for me. If ever I begin to doubt my call to ministry, I have only to remember what happened that night, and my faith is renewed. For the first time in my life I had experienced God not as a vague concept but as an intimately personal Presence.

But that was only the beginning. What happened that night has not been my one-and-only experience of the presence of God, and those three letters are not my only evidence of the providence of God, for my whole life has been filled with experiences that have confirmed over and over again the strengthening presence and providential power of God. With the hindsight of faith I can even see how God was at work in my life long before that night on the Dixie Highway, and long before I ever knew it. I had experienced the providence of God over and over again from my youth, but I had not realized it, and I had not given God the credit.

The light first dawned for me in Daytona Beach, Florida. It took a while to penetrate my secular mind, but after three letters in a row I was, as I have said, beginning to get the message. I was starting to see everything from a faith perspective and to evaluate everything in relation to my call to ministry. I had discovered that God can provide even in material ways when one sincerely seeks to do God's will and puts one's trust in God.

God's providential acts are the confirming evidence of God's call, and I was getting all kinds of confirmation. The three letters gave both Margie and me confidence that God would open the way for us to go to seminary. There was little else we could do about it in Florida, except to pray, and that we were doing in earnest.

Margie and I had started praying together for the first time after learning that our son Ricky had leukemia. We kept hoping for a miracle of healing, and two of our well-meaning friends had come to us in the early stages with the message that if our faith in God were strong enough, Ricky would be healed. We had tried hard to believe that, but somehow the merciful God did not allow us to make a work out of faith. We knew enough to end all of our prayers with the words, "Nevertheless, thy will be done," and we prayed that God would give us the faith to believe, come what may, that God's will is right and good. We were grateful that Ricky's lengthy remission was continuing in Florida with no signs of abatement.

After my Damascus Road experience, our prayers took on a different dimension. We were now thinking in terms of what God wanted of us, rather than in terms of what we wanted from God. We were still praying for Ricky to be healed, of course, but we were also asking for God's guidance, as we wondered how we were going to do what I had been called to do.

One thing was certain: We would not know the answer to that question until I had written a few seminaries, and that I could not do until we returned to Baltimore. For that reason we were all the more anxious to begin our long drive home. It was a strenuous trip, as I had to do advance publicity work in several of the cities where the Orioles were scheduled to play exhibition games on their way north. Margie and the children were even more relieved than I, when we finally arrived home on March 31, Ricky's birthday.

It took me more than a week to catch up on my work at the office, so that it was not until April 8 that I finally was able to get to the task of writing the four seminaries Dr. Poteat had recommended. As Margie and I were discussing the content of the letter that evening, an idea suddenly came to me from out of the blue. Margie immediately noticed my change of expression. "What are you thinking about?" she asked.

"I just thought of another place I should write," I replied, without telling her the name.

"Where?"

"The most obvious place of all. I don't know why neither one of us has thought of it before this."

"Where? Where?" Margie demanded, impatiently.

"Princeton Seminary!"

"Of course! Princeton Seminary! Why didn't we think of it?"

For the life of me, I'll never know why I had not thought of Princeton Theological Seminary, whose main campus is nestled between the graduate school campus and the undergraduate campus of Princeton University, my own alma mater! I had walked across the seminary campus many times en route to basketball practice in the seminary's gymnasium. Princeton University's Dillon Gymnasium was being rebuilt after being destroyed by fire, and the seminary had kindly allowed our varsity basketball squad to use the seminary gym. Despite my daily contact with the seminary campus, I had no other connection with that institution. The university community and the seminary community were two different worlds, as far as I was concerned.

I was certainly aware, however, that there was a seminary in Princeton. Why, then, had I not thought of it when I was trying to think of places to write? It is even more remarkable that Margie had never thought of it either, especially since Princeton was her hometown! Nor had Dr. Poteat suggested it. For whatever reason, the idea of applying to Princeton Theological Seminary had never occurred to me.

I decided to write exactly the same letter on plain stationery to each of the five seminaries, stating my desire to study for the ministry, and indicating only that I was a World War II veteran with a BA degree, that I was married and had three children, and that I would need some financial aid.

As we were speculating about what kinds of responses we would receive, and wondering if there was anyone else whose advice I should seek, we simultaneously thought of my cousin Maurice Armstrong, a Presbyterian minister in Philadelphia. Maurice was my father's first cousin, and hence my first cousin once removed. In age he was almost exactly halfway between Dad and me, and I thought of him almost as an older brother, as well as a good friend. Maurice and his family had been very kind to me during the year I spent in the Naval Supply Corps midshipmen-officers' course at the Harvard Business School during World War II. Their house in Belmont, a suburb of Boston, became a home away from home for me, and I welcomed every opportunity to enjoy one of Irene Armstrongs' delicious meals.

By the time I returned from overseas, Maurice had joined the faculty at Ursinus College outside Philadelphia. He had moved with his family to Manoa, Pennsylvania, which, along with Merwood Park and several other communities, composed the post-office district of Havertown, Pennsylvania. In the summer of 1947, while I was a member of the Lancaster baseball team in the Interstate League, I telephoned Maurice and Irene to tell them that I had fallen in love with a beautiful young woman, whom I wanted very much for them to meet.

The opportunity for that finally occurred near the end of the baseball season, when the Lancaster Red Roses were playing in Wilmington, Delaware. Following our night game, I took an early-morning train to Philadelphia, where I had arranged to meet Margie, who came down from Princeton. We boarded a suburban train for Wynnewood, Pennsylvania. Maurice met us at the station and drove us to their home in nearby Manoa. We had a delicious lunch and a delightful visit, during which my cousins were completely captivated by Margie and excited by the news of our engagement.

I had fallen in love with a beautiful young woman named Margaret Frances Childs. She was a freshman at Wellesley, when this picture was taken. We started dating the following year, when I was a midshipman at the Naval Supply Corps School at Harvard.

After that visit, Margie understood why I felt so close to these cousins about whom she had heard so much. A few weeks later, as the plans for our wedding were taking shape, she was as eager as I to have Maurice take part in the service, along with her grandfather and the pastor of her family's church in Princeton, where she had been confirmed and to which she still belonged. Little did Margie and I know then that four years later we would be living less than a mile from Maurice and his family! We spent many enjoyable social evenings with them and became even closer during the three years that we shared the Havertown post office.

It was no surprise, therefore, that as we were now searching our minds for someone to whom we could turn for advice, we should both think of Maurice. He was the obvious and logical person, for he was not only a minister but someone for whom both Margie and I had immense respect as well as affection. That it should suddenly seem clear and right to confide in Maurice and seek his advice at that time our faith now perceives to have been divine guidance.

That same night I called Maurice on the telephone and told him I needed his advice about a personal matter. I asked if I could drive up to see him as soon as it was convenient for him. "How about tomorrow? Why don't you come for dinner and spend the night with us." That was an invitation I was delighted to accept! With opening day just around the corner, I was absolutely swamped, but it would be even worse after the regular season began. For me sooner was better than later.

The next day I drove up to Havertown late in the afternoon, arriving shortly before dinnertime. Maurice and Irene, whom I had not seen for many months, greeted me warmly. Their three daughters were home. The oldest, Sheila Hollowell, was there with her toddler son Rory. Christine was now eighteen, and Ainslie, the youngest, was eight. Their son, Jock, was now working in Florida. It felt like old times to be sitting at the table again with these cousins whom I dearly loved. I noticed, however, that Maurice and Irene were unusually quiet. The young people chatted freely and responded readily to

Three years later, following Margie's graduation from Wellesley and my return from overseas and subsequent graduation from Princeton, we became engaged.

my questions about their activities, but the laughter and good humor that had always characterized our conversation was strangely missing. Maurice maintained an uncommonly serious though not-unpleasant demeanor throughout the meal. After dinner Irene excused us from our customary dishwashing chore, and Maurice and I retired to his den, the walls of which were covered from floor to ceiling with shelves of books. We sat in two well-worn but comfortable chairs away from his crowded desk.

"I've been looking forward so much to talking with you, Maurice. I really need your advice . . ."

Maurice was gazing at me intently, with a look of genuine concern, as I continued. "I hardly know where to begin, except to say right up front that I've decided to go into the ministry, and I want to talk with you about it. I have so many questions to ask you . . ."

The expression on Maurice's face changed instantly. "Oh, Dick," he said with a great sigh, "I'm so relieved! I was sure you were going to tell me that you and Margie were having marital troubles!"

"Oh, so that's why you and Irene seemed so glum at the dinner table tonight! I'm sorry I caused you any concern. No, Margie and I love each other more than ever, and she is with me 100 percent in this matter. We've been talking about little else for weeks."

Maurice was all smiles now. "That's wonderful, Dick! I want to hear all about it. When did you decide? How did it happen?"

I described as well as I could my experience in the car that momentous night in Daytona Beach and the events leading up to it. I told him how I had decided just a few days before to make baseball my permanent career, and how totally unprepared I was for such a visit from God. "I still can't believe God would call the likes of me into the ministry."

"You're not the first person who ever felt that way, Dick. God calls all kinds of people. And God uses whatever talents and abilities a person has to offer."

"It's not that, Maurice. It's just that I don't consider myself to be very religious. And I have to confess that I even feel uneasy around people who talk about Jesus all the time . . ."

"So do I."

I was relieved to hear that, but I went on to explain: "Oh, I don't fault them for being what they are and believing what they believe. It's just that they seem to be insensitive and sometimes even arrogant about it, and they turn other people off. I don't want to be like that. I'm not comfortable with people who make a display of their religion. Do you know what I mean?"

"Indeed I do. I feel the same way."

"I call myself a Christian, but I wonder if I really am. I don't know what to think about Jesus."

"It's no sin to admit you have doubts, Dick. Every honest person does."

"But can I go to into the ministry feeling the way I do?"

"You have plenty of time to wrestle with these kinds of questions. The important point is that you believe in God, and God has called you into the ministry. The God who has called you will give you the faith you need. God wouldn't have called you otherwise."

"That gives me hope, but we'll have to wait and see what kind of response I receive from the seminaries I wrote to. I haven't heard from anyone yet." I went on to tell Maurice about the letters I had written and mentioned the names of the five seminaries.

"Princeton seems like the logical choice, Dick."

"That's a Presbyterian seminary, isn't it? Does it make any difference that I'm an Episcopalian?"

"Not at all. The student body is very ecumenical. There are many denominations represented. However, I do think you and Margie need to find a church in your present community and transfer your membership there. Are you both still on the rolls of a church?"

"I really don't know. It has been years since I've had any contact with St. Thomas. I think Margie is still on the rolls of her church, but we never hear from them either. We need to find out."

"Getting back to Princeton Seminary, why don't you make an appointment to talk to the president of the seminary, Dr. John Mackay? He's a Scot, and a wonderful man. I'm sure he'd be very sympathetic to your situation."

I had never heard of John Mackay, and I was a bit doubtful about approaching the president of the seminary. But I thanked Maurice for his suggestion, and said I'd think about it, concluding with, "I guess there would be no harm in asking for an appointment to see Dr. Mackay."

"I have a feeling you'll be glad you did."

We chatted for quite a while longer about many things relating to my call to ministry and what lay ahead. Maurice again stressed the importance of our joining a local church as soon as possible. He answered many of my questions about what I had to look forward to in seminary and beyond. I hung on every word, as he talked about the satisfactions as well as the challenges of being a minister and shared some of his own experiences in the churches he had served. Maurice's positive reaction to my becoming a minister was just the encouragement I needed, and another welcome confirmation of my call.

"You have been so helpful, Maurice," I said, as we were turning out the lights in his study. "Thank you so much for tonight. It has been wonderful! And I appreciate your understanding of my situation and why we haven't yet told our parents or anyone else about my call. I'm afraid my folks would be very upset. That's why Margie and I want to have a better idea of what is in store for us, before we spring this news on them. I just can't say, 'I'm thinking about going into the ministry,' although Margie's folks would probably be thrilled. As for the Orioles and the general public, I'm not telling a soul until I'm accepted by some seminary. At that point I'll announce that I'm resigning as public relations director in order to study for the ministry. Anyway, thanks again!"

The next morning, as we lingered at the breakfast table after the young people had all left the house, I told Irene that I was planning to go to seminary, and that is what I had wanted to talk with Maurice about. I assured her, with a knowing glance at Maurice, that everything was fine with Margie and me. "I'm sorry I caused you some concern; but, you see, we haven't told a soul about my desire to become a minister, not even our parents. Maurice can fill you in on how this all came about. Anyway, I want to thank both of you for all your help. And thank you again, Irene, for that delicious dinner last night and for breakfast this morning. It was so good to be with you folks again."

We said our goodbyes, and a few minutes later I was back on City Line Avenue, heading for Baltimore. As I was driving along I found myself getting more and more excited about the thought of going back to school to study for the ministry, at Princeton Seminary or wherever it turned out to be.

That feeling was the first evidence of the transforming power of the Holy Spirit. Although I could not have expressed it that way at the time, I was quite aware of what a tremendous change in me that very feeling represented. I can remember laughing about it to myself in the car. To think that I would be excited about going back to school—I, who never wanted to see another textbook, write another term paper, take another exam, or listen to another lecture! When I graduated from college I declared to any and all interested persons that I would never consider any career that involved my going to graduate school.

That had been distressing news to Margie's parents, who would by far have preferred that their daughter marry a teacher or a doctor or a journalist, or someone in a more respectable occupation than the one I was heading for. Their understanding of a profession did not include professional baseball! A distinguished professor of political science at Princeton University, Margie's father time and again would ask me if I might not consider being a college professor. "It's a wonderful profession, Dick," he would always say, "and it would be a most satisfying life for you and Margie."

"I'm sure it would be, Dr. Childs," I would reply, "but I have no interest whatsoever in an academic career. I want to see if I can play some professional baseball, and then I hope to find a job in the front office." Arthur Ehlers, who had signed me to play in the Athletics' minor league system, had indicated that there would be a front office job for me with one of their minor league teams at the end of the season, if I would be interested. I was!

Dr. and Mrs. Childs were the most gracious of people, and I respected them greatly. They were genuinely pleased when Margie and I announced

Willa and Harwood Childs, outside their home in Princeton. A distinguished professor of political science at Princeton University and an expert in the field of propaganda, Professor Childs was one of the first in America to speak out publicly and forcefully against the menace of Nazism. That conviction was the result of his extensive research in Germany in 1931–32 and 1937, including a three-hour interview with Hitler, while on a Guggenheim Fellowship.

But to Ellen and Ricky and their other adoring grandchildren they are just Grampy and Granmama.

our engagement. But I had the feeling they were somewhat less-than-enthusiastic, if not embarrassed, to tell their friends what their future son-in-law was doing. They knew nothing about baseball, and their image of a career in professional sports was anything but positive.

Their negative impression had been dramatically reinforced one August evening in 1947, when Margie, her father, and her younger sister, Martha, came to the Trenton ballpark to see the Lancaster Red Roses play the Trenton Giants. Lancaster and Trenton were battling for a spot in the playoffs. That was the first professional baseball game Dr. Childs had ever seen. He was the only man in the stands wearing a coat and tie, and he looked very professorial (and very out of place) with his prematurely white hair and his dark suit. I had told them that I would not be pitching that night, but they wanted to come anyway.

As it turned out, I was sorry they came. *Mortified* would be a more accurate description, for the game was interrupted that night by a free-for-all between the two teams. It became rather ugly, as the fans began throwing things at our players. With the help of some local policemen, and after ejecting a few of the perpetrators of the fracas, the umpires finally got the game under control. That was not the kind of introduction to baseball I had had in mind for my future father-in-law!

No wonder he had worries about the career I had chosen. His gentle cajoling was of no avail, however. I was determined to accept whatever position Arthur Ehlers offered me. As it turned out, I was appointed business manager of the Portsmouth (Ohio) Baseball Club in the Ohio-Indiana League. I had several weeks of training in the fall and early winter of 1947, including a conference for business managers, before assuming the responsibilities of organizing a new professional baseball franchise in Portsmouth. Margie and I moved to that Ohio River city in February 1948, following our honeymoon.

No privacy on our honeymoon! The French Canadian newspaper *La Patrie* sent a reporter to interview us in our hotel room. The owner of the International League Montreal Royals entertained us royally during our stay in his city. After returning to Princeton for a brief visit with Margie's folks, we loaded our car and headed for Portsmouth, Ohio, where our exciting baseball adventure began the moment we arrived in town.

January 31, 1948, the newlyweds, outside Princeton University Chapel

Lying at the confluence of the Ohio and Sciota rivers, Portsmouth is prone to floods, and we had one in March 1948. All of us in our training camp, including scouts, managers, and ninety players, joined the local citizens in their valiant but unsuccessful efforts to prevent what was for most of us our first experience of flooding. Margie and I were impressed by the equalizing effect this common disaster has upon the residents of this historic river city.

Our excitement mounted as we came upon the first road sign to Portsmouth, where we'll be looking for a furnished apartment to rent.

The 1948 Portsmouth Athletics were literally rained out of the pennant on the last day of the season, when the heavens opened up in the fourth inning, ending the game and nullifying their sizeable lead. Instead of winning by a half game, they finished second by the same margin.

Attending the ball games became the thing to do in Portsmouth! It helped that we had plenty of free parking.

Our disappointment at being nosed our of the league championship was somewhat mollified by the fact the we led the Ohio-Indiana League in attendance, as the local fans poured out in great numbers in support of their new professional franchise.

July 25, 1949—it's Connie Mack Day in Portsmouth. Art Ehlers, Farm Director of the Philadelphia Athletics; George Trautman, Commission of Minor League Baseball (sixty leagues); Connie Mack, President and Manager of the A's; Frank Colley, President of the Ohio-Indiana League; and I were honored guests a luncheon hosted by the mayor of Portsmouth. It was followed that afternoon by an exciting parade down the main street of Portsmouth, as the city turned out to cheer the "Grand Old Man of Baseball."

A Sense of Being Called

Right: Margie and Connie Mack pause for a pose just before the big parade.

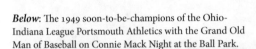

Below: The 1949 soon-to-be-champions of the Ohio-Indiana League Portsmouth Athletics with the Grand Old Man of Baseball on Connie Mack Night at the Ball Park.

Left: Here she is, Miss Ellen Childs Armstrong, in her basket. She was born on March 24, 1949, and at six weeks she could laugh uproariously, an early sign of her present sense of humor. Ellen attended every home game that season—in her basket! There were plenty of willing volunteers looking out for her. No wonder Ellen became and is still such a baseball fan.

Right: Two members of the Portsmouth team were hospitalized, nine others were treated and discharged with minor injuries, following a serious bus accident in the middle of the 1949 season. Despite the accident, the Portsmouth A's, with help from other Philadelphia Athletics farm clubs, went on to win the Ohio-Indiana League pennant.

Lynnewood Gardens as it looks today. Responding to a full-page ad we saw in the Philadelphia Inquirer we showed up at the rental office here on the very first morning it opened and were the first customers to sign up for an apartment, which we moved into on the day it was ready for occupancy.

We look back on our Portsmouth days as one of the happiest periods of our life together. Those two seasons were formative for me, as I had ample opportunity to use every talent and skill I possessed in running that minor league franchise.

Despite a serious bus accident in which nine of our players were injured, two seriously, we won the pennant in our second year, and despite the area's economic woes, we had another good year at the gate. I was hoping to move up in the Athletics organization, but to my surprise and great joy, I never had to ask for a promotion, for I was invited to submit a proposal for establishing a public relations department for the major league Athletics. I had put together a plan featuring a yearlong celebration of Connie Mack's fiftieth anniversary with the Philadelphia Athletics, and on the strength of that was given the job. We moved our belongings to Margie's parents' large faculty home in Princeton, and for several weeks I commuted to work at Shibe Park. Eventually we rented an apartment in Lynnewood Gardens, a newly developed complex on the northern boundary of Philadelphia.

These were the memories flashing through my mind as I drove south on Route 1 to Baltimore that sunny Friday morning, April 15, 1955. Our life in baseball had been so exciting and my work so fulfilling that I had never had the slightest inclination ever to go to graduate school, and I adamantly refused to listen to any suggestion to that effect. But now that long-held aversion to any kind of graduate school had completely vanished. How utterly astounding! The God who had called me into the ministry had transformed that aversion into an eager expectation. It was one of the many mini-miracles I have experienced along the pathway of faith.

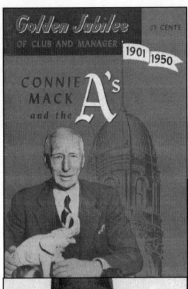

Left: In addition to the pictures and stats of the players, the 1950 *Athletics Yearbook* featured the history of Connie Mack's fifty years as manager of the A's, during which his teams won five World Series and eight American League championships. The excitement of the early-season celebrations that year was offset by the A's disappointing performance on the field, even as the pennant-bound Phillies, our tenants, forever remembered as the Whiz Kids, were capturing the imagination of Philadelphia baseball fans.

Above; Early one morning in West Palm Beach Mr. Mack agreed to don a uniform for the first time in fifty years and pose for our club photographer. I put out a press release under the heading "A's Sign New Rookie." The wire services jumped on the story and it must have appeared in every newspaper in North America!

Above: March 1950. This is the way Mr. Mack usually dressed! He was a fashion plate on or off the field. We're standing in front of the A's dugout during a workout at Wright Field in West Palm Beach.

I was so busy with my own thoughts that the drive home from Havertown seemed to take no time at all. Margie was expecting me home by lunchtime that day, and I made it with a half hour to spare. Even as we hugged, she was a torrent of questions: "How did it go? What did Maurice say? Was he surprised? Did he have any suggestions? What was his first reaction? . . ."

"We had a wonderful talk. I'm so glad we both thought of Maurice. When I told him why I needed to talk with him, his first reaction, believe it or not, was one of relief! He had been afraid that you and I were having problems and that I was coming for marriage counseling!"

"Oh, dear!" exclaimed Margie, laughingly.

I then proceeded to give her a detailed description of the dinner Irene had prepared, the strained table talk, and a verbatim account of my conversation with Maurice, up to the point of his suggesting that I try to see the president of Princeton Theological Seminary, Dr. John Mackay.

The name was hardly out of my mouth when Margie exclaimed excitedly, "I know Dr. Mackay! My sister Betty Ann and I overlapped with the Mackay children in high school. My parents and the Mackays know each other well. They're good friends."

I stared open mouthed at Margie. "That's unbelievable! Maurice suggests that I talk to a man I never heard of, and I come home to discover that my wife went to school with his children!"

God was about to open another door.

4

This Is Providential!

The next few days brought letters in the mail from four of the five semi-naries I had written, including one from Princeton Seminary. Each of the seminaries encouraged me to apply, and indicated there might be a small amount of scholarship aid available, plus various fieldwork possibilities.

Margie and I were grateful for the tone of the letters and for the offers of financial help, but we wondered how we would manage on the small amounts of aid that were mentioned. The letter from Princeton was signed by Dr. J. Donald Butler, acting dean of the seminary. He enclosed a catalogue and an application for admission and suggested that if I was interested I should return the application promptly. He indicated that I would need a transcript of my undergraduate academic record and a letter of recommendation from my pastor. The latter requirement was a matter of concern to me since I had not attended St. Thomas Episcopal Church for such a long time.

I was especially interested, however, in the third paragraph of Dr. Butler's letter, which read as follows:

> In answer to your inquiry concerning scholarship aid, you can count on receiving at least $200 a year in scholarship aid from the funds of the Seminary, provided you need this amount. Shortly after your matriculation, you will fill out a scholarship application form on which you will make out an itemized budget, and the President will discuss this with you. If, after exhausting all sources

of income, you cannot balance your budget, the President will discuss the matter of further aid with you. He is always ready to stand
behind a worthy student who is in need.

The references to the president were the unintended inducement I
needed to do what my cousin Maurice had suggested! Margie and I concluded that there was nothing to lose and everything to gain in trying to see
Dr. Mackay in person.

But how should I approach him? Should I simply call his secretary
and ask for an appointment? Ordinarily that is what I would have done, but
Margie suggested a better way: "I think your chances of seeing Dr. Mackay
would be better if my father called to make the appointment. He wouldn't
have to go into any detailed explanation. All he'd have to say is, 'My son-in-
law is thinking about going into the ministry. Would you be willing to talk
with him about it?' Then if Dr. Mackay says yes, Daddy can talk with him
about a date. How do you feel about that?"

"It sounds good to me. That means, of course, we'll have to tell your
folks about my call. Maybe it's time we did that anyway."

I felt absolutely no reluctance in saying that. In fact, the thought of
letting Margie's parents in on our big secret actually brought an immediate sense not just of relief but of great joy. We decided to call them on the
telephone that evening and tell them all that had been going on in our lives.
Knowing that Dr. Childs was an elder in the First Presbyterian Church
of Princeton, I could hardly wait to hear his reaction to the news that his
son-in-law wanted to become a minister and to the idea of my applying to
Princeton Theological Seminary. I was sure that Grampy and Granmama,
as they were now called by all of us, would be thrilled at the possibility of
our moving to Princeton, if everything could be worked out.

We talked less on the telephone and corresponded more in those days.
In recent years I've come to regret that we have exchanged so few letters
with our children since their college years. Because we have communicated
mostly by telephone, we lack the historical record of family affairs that correspondence provides. But in the earlier days of our married life, telephone
calls were for special occasions, and this was one. With the use of exten-
sion phones on both ends, our telephone visits with Margie's parents were
almost always four-way conversations, and this was no exception.

After the usual pleasantries, Margie set the stage: "The reason we called
is that Dick has some exciting news to share with you." Without pausing I
continued, "I've decided to become a minister!"

My announcement was greeted first with stunned silence on the other end of the line. "Did you say 'minister'?" asked Dr. Childs.

"Yes. As soon as I am admitted to a seminary, I'm going to resign from the Orioles in order to study for the ministry." I went on to relate how I had come to that point.

"That is exciting news!" commented Margie's mother.

"Yes, it is," agreed Dr. Childs, less than enthusiastically. "I think it's wonderful that you want to go into the ministry, Dick, but do you think this is the right time? You have a good job there with the Orioles, and Ricky is receiving the finest medical care at Johns Hopkins Hospital. I don't think you should be too quick to give all that up. Having to move might be terribly hard on Ricky. Maybe God wants you to wait a while. And maybe that's why those seminaries responded the way they did. How would you support your family if you quit your job?"

I was completely unprepared for that cautious reaction from my father-in-law, who I thought would have been overjoyed by our news. Instead, Elder Childs raised very practical, worldly-wise questions that revealed that he was harboring some serious reservations about my decision to study for the ministry.

"We've been wrestling with these very questions," I replied. "But Margie and I feel that if God has called me into the ministry, everything will work out, as far as Ricky is concerned. He's in God's hands. I'm sure we'll find a good doctor for him wherever we are. We'll cross that bridge when we get there. The point is, I believe with all my heart that God wants me to be a minister. It's not really my decision. It's something I must do."

"I understand, Dick. All I'm saying is, maybe this is not the best time. God knows you have a family to support and a child with leukemia."

"I appreciate your concern, and that's why we're exploring some possibilities. Frankly speaking, I don't know yet how I can go to seminary and support my family at the same time without substantial scholarship aid. In that connection, my cousin Maurice Armstrong thinks it would be a good idea for me to talk with Dr. Mackay at Princeton Seminary, and Margie and I were hoping, since you know him, that you would call him to ask if he would be willing to see me. Maurice said Dr. Mackay is a very compassionate man and may be sympathetic to our situation."

"I'm sure he would be, Dick. And of course I'll call him for you. It certainly wouldn't do any harm to talk with him. When could you come up to see him?"

"Any day next week, since the Orioles will be on the road again. Wednesday would be my first choice."

"I'll call him tomorrow."

"Wonderful!"

Margie's parents seemed to become more receptive to the idea as we talked. After we hung up, Margie and I agreed that we should tell my parents also. We decided to wait, however, until after I had seen Dr. Mackay. I dreaded telling my dad, for I was afraid that he would be totally shocked by and opposed to the idea of my becoming a minister. Unlike Margie's parents, mine were neither members nor attenders of any church. I felt I had to present my father with a fait accompli.

Two days later Dr. Childs called back to inform me that Dr. Mackay would be able to see me at noon the following Wednesday, April 20. He had also made an appointment for me to talk that same morning with the Rev. Dr. John Bodo, pastor of the First Presbyterian Church of Princeton. "He's a very wise man, Dick, and he relates well to young adults. I think he might be able to give you some sound advice."

"That's great! I'd enjoy talking with your pastor. Thank you for setting up those appointments. I really appreciate it." How grateful I was for Margie's father and mother, who had become like second parents to me.

At ten o'clock the following Wednesday morning I was waiting outside the pastor's study at the First Presbyterian Church. Margie's mother had invited me to spend Tuesday night at their house, to avoid the pressure of my having to drive up to Princeton early Wednesday morning. More important, I had had a most meaningful visit with Margie's parents that night and was tremendously moved by their concern and support, as we discussed in depth the implications of my call.

I had no idea what to expect from my conversation with Dr. Bodo. After receiving me warmly, he began the conversation by inviting me to tell him why I wanted to go to seminary. As I nervously began to share my Damascus Road experience and the related events that had transpired since then, Dr. Bodo smiled and nodded encouragingly from time to time, so that I soon felt very much at ease. When I had finished, he sat with his head tilted to one side, silently pondering my lengthy reply to his question.

Then he smiled, and looking me straight in the eye, he commented in a very thoughtful tone, "There is no doubt that God has called you into ministry, Dick. But what makes you think you have to be an ordained clergyman in order to have a ministry? How do you know God isn't calling you to be an active lay Christian? You can have a powerful ministry as a layman. What an opportunity you have in professional baseball, especially with the work you have been doing in radio and television! Once you get that 'Rev.' in front of your name, you won't be running in the same circles. You're in a highly visible role now, with a fantastic opportunity to reach people and to influence people. As a layperson you can have a much greater impact. In short, I think you're going in the right direction, but you're on the wrong track!"

There's no way to describe my reaction to Dr. Bodo's advice, except to say that I felt as if a horse had kicked me in the stomach—not because I thought his advice was preposterous, but because it was so plausible. The suggestion that God wanted me to become an active Christian layman was an entirely new thought for me, and I knew I had to take it seriously. It actually made much more sense than for someone who was not even an active member of a church to become a clergyman.

But in my heart I earnestly believed God wanted me to be a minister, and for me that meant being a pastor of a church. It did not matter to me that I had a very limited understanding of what that entailed. It was enough that I at least knew it meant preaching to a congregation. Yet here was a man of God, who I had to assume was better qualified than I to interpret the will of God, telling me I had misunderstood God's call.

Such were my thoughts, as our conversation continued, until finally it was time for me to leave. I thanked Dr. Bodo for seeing me, but I did not tell him how distressed and depressed I was feeling as I left his office.

I wonder if any passersby could have known my inner turmoil as I walked almost aimlessly across the university campus toward the seminary. Looking back on that experience I can honestly say that I wanted with all my heart to do God's will, but now all of a sudden I was filled with uncertainty. I was ready to go anywhere God wanted me to go, do anything God wanted me to do, be whatever God wanted me to be. I just was not sure what God wanted. I was praying from the time I left the church until I walked into the administration building at the seminary, imploring God for an answer. If I had known the biblical expression, I would have been saying, "Lord, show me a sign!"

Sitting literally and figuratively with my back to the wall opposite the large desk of Dr. Mackay's rather preoccupied secretary, I began to ask myself, 'What am I doing here?' I felt entirely out of place, as if my wanting to go to seminary was a huge mistake. I resisted the impulse to excuse myself and walk out. I was ready to go home and give it all up as an impossible pipe dream. "Maybe Dr. Bodo was right," I said to myself. "Maybe what I should do is become active in a church and try to be a better Christian. There really is no need for me to waste Dr. Mackay's time. Still, he was kind enough to agree to see me, so I guess I'm obligated to keep the appointment."

In the midst of my brooding, I was suddenly aware of a voice saying, "The president will see you now, Mr. Armstrong." The secretary was standing before me, gesturing toward the open door to my left. I rose to my feet and walked into a spacious room as she closed the door behind me. Standing behind a large mahogany desk was a man in a three-piece navy-blue suit, with snow-white hair and a beaming smile. Never had I seen such a radiant countenance. I felt as if I were standing on holy ground and meeting St. Peter himself!

Dr. Mackay greeted me with a firm handshake and invited me to sit in a leather-covered armchair away from his desk and diagonally adjacent to the matching chair into which he had moved from the high-backed swivel chair behind his desk. "Dr. Childs has told me very little about you, except that you are thinking about going into the ministry. Why don't you tell me about yourself? How did you come to this decision?"

"Thank you for your interest, Dr. Mackay, and for fitting me into your busy schedule. I must admit I'm not sure in my own mind what God wants me to do, but I had a remarkable experience several weeks ago, which I'm still trying to understand." I went on to tell what had happened to me that night in the car

The Rev. Dr. John Alexander Mackay played a key role in my call to and preparation for ministry.

and how sure I had been until this very morning that God wanted me to become a minister, serving a congregation. That meant my having to quit my job in order to go to seminary. Then I told him about my conversation with Dr. Bodo, and why I was now uncertain about what God wanted me to do. "You must understand, Dr. Mackay, that I know very little about these things. I don't have the vocabulary to describe what has happened to me or the theology to explain it. I'm a public relations man, not a theologian. All I know is, God wants me to be a minister."

Dr. Mackay had been listening the whole while with his fingertips pressed together and the kindliest expression on his face. When I had finished speaking, he grinned broadly and gleefully uttered what I later came to know was one of his favorite expressions: "Oh, boys! Oh, boys! This is providential!" he exclaimed with great enthusiasm. "The trustees have just authorized me to hire a public relations person for the seminary and now God has sent one into my office! If you would be interested in working for us part-time while going to seminary, I think we could work something out."

Was I interested! There was God's answer. There was the sign I was looking for. Let the world call it a remarkable coincidence. I knew my prayers had been answered. It was, as Dr. Mackay had said, providential. I made no effort to hide my excitement: "I certainly would be interested, Dr. Mackay!"

"I'll have to talk this over with Dr. Quay, the vice president of the seminary, for he's the one you'd be working for. He'll want to talk with you, of course. You'll also need the approval of the development committee of the trustees. Could you send me your resume and some samples of your work that I can show them? They will accept Dr. Quay's and my recommendation, but we have to go through the formalities, you know. I'll have Dr. Quay get in touch with you about arranging a date. He's not in today. Could you come up to Princeton to see him, and to discuss the terms of your employment? You'll also need to apply for admission. I suggest you try to see Dean Butler this afternoon before you return to Baltimore. I don't know whether or not he's available."

"I'd like very much to see Dean Butler. I wrote to him several days ago and received a nice reply. He sent me an application form, which I have not yet completed. I was hoping to be able to talk with you before deciding whether or not to apply for admission. After talking with you, I certainly do want to apply!"

I was an Episcopalian when I entered Dr. Mackay's office. I knew nothing about predestination or the doctrine of election. But I had the definite feeling that things were moving according to a wonderful plan— God's plan! I tried to express something to that effect to Dr. Mackay, but my words fell far short. He knew I was grateful, and I do believe he was as excited about finding a public relations person as I was about becoming a student at Princeton Theological Seminary.

After leaving Dr. Mackay's office, I went to the other end of the administration building to make an appointment to see Dean Butler, but I discovered that both he and his secretary were out to lunch. I then walked back to

106 Broadmead for a late lunch with Dr. and Mrs. Childs, who were eagerly waiting to hear all about my morning in Princeton. After my detailed account of the visits with Dr. Bodo and President Mackay, my parents-in-law were much more positive about my going to seminary than they had been at first. They reiterated their concerns about Ricky, but I left them with the feeling that they both understood and supported my call to be a minister.

That afternoon I walked back to the seminary in hopes of seeing Dean Butler, who was in a meeting. I waited as long as I could, but I finally had to leave without seeing him, in order to catch my train to Baltimore.

When I arrived home by taxi that evening, Margie was full of questions, as I knew she would be. I spared no details in recounting every conversation almost word for word, and what I was feeling at the time. My excitement was exceeded only by my amazement at the way things seemed to be working out, and both feelings were intensified as I shared the entire experience with Margie. She was as excited and amazed as I was. As we talked long into the night, we both concluded that we should wait no longer to tell my parents even though we had no definite word from Princeton Seminary and probably would not for many days.

The next day I slipped into my father's office and closed the door behind me. "Have you got a few minutes, Dad?" I asked. "I need to talk with you." As busy as we both always were, we were never too busy to see each other, but neither one of us ever took advantage of that fact. We had, as I have already stated, an ideal working relationship.

"I have something to tell you, Dad, and I've been waiting for the right time." My father's serious countenance indicated he knew something momentous was about to be unveiled. There was no way I could ease into it, so I jumped in with both feet: "What I want to tell you is that I've decided to resign from the Orioles at the end of the season in order to study for the ministry. I'm not sure yet where we'll be going, but I'm hoping to be able to enter Princeton Theological Seminary in the fall."

I was sure the news would be a terrible blow to my father, because of the beautifully close bond that had developed between us, as we worked side by side for the Orioles. We had always been close, but we had never before worked together professionally. The level of cooperation and trust between us could not have been greater. Not only had my initial fears of working for the same organization as my father not materialized, but the mutual respect and enjoyment we shared as front office colleagues far exceeded anything I could have imagined. The thought of our no longer working together for the Orioles was as painful to me as I imagined it would be for my dad. I was sure he would not be angry, but of course he would be surprised and maybe even hurt. Most of all he would be sad. In any case, I was prepared for the worst.

How wrong I was! When I had dropped the bombshell, Dad said not a word, as his eyes filled with tears. I could not remember ever before having seen my father weep like that. But these were tears of joy, not of sorrow! After a few moments he composed himself, and said "You can't imagine how happy and proud that makes me feel, Dick. You will make a wonderful minister!"

Herbert E. Armstrong (1893–1984). I never knew a person I admired and respected more than I did my dad. He was a man of the highest integrity, an excellent teacher, coach, and leader of men. After teaching and coaching for thirty-one years, he resigned as athletic director and head of the Math Department at McDonogh School to become a front office executive with the International League Orioles. He was retained by the new owners as business manager of the American League Orioles. He also served as president of the Baltimore Orioles Foundation, and president of the Maryland Shrine of Immortals. I can't imagine that anyone ever received more honors and awards from more organizations and institutions than he. The *Sporting News* named him the Minor Leagues' Executive of the Year after he planned and supervised the reconfiguring of the old Memorial Stadium for baseball. That included installing lights for night baseball. The seemingly impossible task was accomplished in ten days!

July 1923. Baseball's first commissioner, Judge Kennesaw Mountain Landis, on his first trip to the East Coast, congratulates Cambridge manager Herb Armstrong (my dad) on their first-place standing in the Eastern Shore League, a proving ground for numerous major league stars. Cambridge that day was playing an all-star team composed of players from the other teams in the league.

Oh, the amazing grace of God! I would have thought that my father's reaction and that of Dr. Childs would have been just the reverse of what they were, but God inspired the right reactions in the right person for my benefit. How much better it was for me to hear the prudent word of caution and practical wisdom from Margie's father, the Presbyterian elder, and the word of encouragement and affirmation from my father, the man of the world. It was just the opposite of what Margie and I expected, and therefore so much more helpful to us.

Dad asked me how I had arrived at my decision, but when I tried to tell him what had happened in the car that night in Daytona Beach, he seemed a bit uncomfortable. "I don't think you need to tell people that part, Dick," he said.

"The point is, Dad, that it really isn't something that I have decided to do on my own. I feel this is something God wants me to do, and I have no choice. It wasn't my idea at all. Not once in my life had I ever thought of becoming a minister before that night. It was a call of God, that's all I can say."

I realized that my story would sound fantastic to an unchurched person like my father, and as I later discovered, to many church people as well. I would have to find a way of answering their 'How did you decide?' question that would make sense to them and still do justice to what had actually happened to me.

I told Dad about my visit to Princeton and the possibility of my doing public relations and fundraising for the seminary to help pay for my education and to support my family. "That would be wonderful," he said, "When will you know?"

"I have to send in the application forms, along with some samples of my work. I don't know how long it will take for the seminary to decide, but I have a definite feeling that I'll be accepted. If and when I am, then I'll announce my intention to resign at the end of the season in order to study for the ministry. Up until now we've told no one except Margie's parents and Maurice and Irene Armstrong. I went to see Maurice to ask his advice, and it was he who suggested I talk with Dr. Mackay. We decided to ask Margie's father to make the appointment for me, because he knows Dr. Mackay. That's when we told them about my decision to become a minister. Margie and I wanted to wait until I'd talked to Dr. Mackay before telling you and Muv. We didn't want to upset you or worry you."

"I understand, Dick. I think it's just wonderful that you want to be a minister. I couldn't be more pleased, and I know Muv will feel the same way."

"Muv" was the name my older brother Herb had given our mother when he was an infant, and she had been stuck with it ever since. When I paid my folks a visit later that evening, Dad had already told her the news. My mother was not in the best of health, but she was well enough to express her pleasure about my becoming a minister. She was even more affirming than Dad, and that made Margie and me very happy, because we did not want to cause her any worry. We talked about the impact on our children, especially Ricky, and discussed when and how I should tell Clarence Miles and others of my decision. Dad agreed that I should wait until I had definitely been admitted to Princeton Seminary.

Before leaving I showed my father a letter that had arrived the day I was in Princeton. It was a beautiful follow-up letter from Maurice, reconfirming my decision and informing me that he had spoken on my behalf to the Rev. Marcus J. Priester, who headed the Presbyterian General Assembly office relating to ministerial candidates. Maurice suggested I make an appointment to see Dr. Priester, whose full title was my first introduction to the jargon of Presbyterian bureaucracy: "Executive Secretary of the Department of Vocation of the Division of Higher Education of the Board of Christian Education of the Presbyterian Church in the United States of America"!

"He is very interested in my account of you," wrote Maurice, "and will write to you soon . . . I feel sure he can arrange some help for you. I hope that before you see him you will have decided on a local church membership. That is the first step."

Even my Episcopal eyes could detect that things were tilting more and more toward the Presbyterian Church. Was I getting a message? The very next day I received a warm letter from Dr. Priester suggesting several possible dates for our getting together. Maurice had alerted him that my schedule made it difficult to come to Philadelphia during his regular office hours, so he had very thoughtfully offered to meet me at his home in Lansdowne, Pennsylvania. I immediately called Dr. Priester on the telephone to say that my family and I would be driving to Havertown en route to Princeton on Friday, April 29, and could swing by to see him that evening, since his home was not far off our route.

In the next few days I managed to squeeze in some time to fill out the admission application form for Princeton Seminary and to put together a packet of work samples for Dr. Mackay. I also wrote to each of the other seminaries to inform them of my decision to apply to Princeton.

This Is Providential!

Late in the afternoon of Friday, April 29, with the Orioles on the road again, Margie, the children, and I piled into the car and headed for Havertown, where we would be spending the night at the home of our dear friends Ruth and Ed Emack. We arrived at Dr. Priester's home in Lansdowne a few minutes before 8:00 p.m., the agreed-upon time. Seeing that the children were tired from our long drive, Dr. Priester insisted that Margie drive on with them to the Emacks'. "I'll bring Dick there after our visit."

The offer was sincere, and it was obvious that he would not take no for an answer. So Margie went on with the children, and I stayed and visited with Marcus Priester for nearly two hours. A pleasant, youngish man with a most engaging personality, he did not fit anybody's image of a stodgy church bureaucrat.

By the time we finished I had a much clearer understanding of the entire candidating process, including the required psychological testing. Dr. Priester supplied me with the lengthy test forms to be completed, along with other helpful background materials. Regarding financial aid he told me that there were modest scholarship grants available from the Department of Vocations, for Presbyterian candidates. He also suggested that I write to the Rockefeller Theological Fellowship Program, which gave grants to underwrite a year the seminary education of worthy students who wanted to explore the possibility of a ministerial calling. "You would not be eligible for one of their fellowships, Dick, because you have already made the decision to go into the ministry. But they may be able to offer some suggestions. Anyway, it's worth a try. Their office is right there in Princeton."

"That's a good suggestion. I'll look into it."

Then, anticipating the question I was sure he would ask, I explained the situation concerning our church membership and said that we had just about decided to join the Presbyterian church where we had been worshiping. Dr. Priester was nodding appreciatively.

We continued our conversation on the way to the Emacks', who just happened to be Presbyterians! It was ten o'clock, when we pulled into their

April 11, 1954. Ruth and Ed Emack with Margie. We were in Atlantic City for a weekend engagement of the Suburban Squires. The Emacks lived less than a mile from us and had been immensely kind and helpful to us in countless ways. We knew our secret was safe with them.

driveway. As I waved goodbye to Dr. Priester, I was feeling very comfortable with the thought of becoming a Presbyterian, and I was eager to tell Margie all that I had learned. After the welcoming round of hugs, the Emacks and the Armstrongs had one of our late-night conversations. A sly exchange of glances between Margie and me was the signal to let Ed and Ruth in on our secret.

They were such good friends that it would have been too hard not to tell them, in view of my visit that evening with Dr. Priester and our destination in the morning. We knew our secret was safe with them, and we hoped that they would not have to keep it very long.

We left for Princeton bright and early the next morning. And after dropping off Margie, the children, and our suitcases at 106 Broadmead, I drove back to the seminary campus in the hope that President Mackay and Dean Butler might be in their offices on Saturday morning. Neither one was, so I left the packet of materials and my accompanying letter to Dr. Mackay at the switchboard. Later that afternoon I was able to reach Dean Butler on the telephone at home. Since I had missed him on my earlier visit to the seminary, and since my schedule would prevent me from returning for another month, the dean very kindly agreed to interview me at his home that evening.

It turned out to be a most enjoyable meeting. I was impressed that he could receive so cordially a potential student who was interrupting his Saturday evening. Dr. Butler had heard something of my situation from President Mackay, but it was apparent and proper that he wanted to form his own opinion about this Episcopalian latecomer. I handed him a manila folder containing my completed application, along with the required fee and the four head shots. Taking out the application, the dean proceeded to read it, nodding his head from time to time.

When he had finished reading, he said, as he placed it back in the folder, "We'll try to get you an answer as soon as possible, but it will probably be a month to six weeks before we decide one way or the other. I can't assure you at this time that you will be accepted, but I feel there is a reasonably good chance that you will be accepted."

I assured the dean that I understood my employment at the seminary was contingent upon my being accepted as a student. He then asked about my undergraduate work at Princeton University, as well as my graduate work at the Harvard Business School. "We'll need your transcripts as soon as possible, along with the letters of recommendation, including one from your pastor. I understand you are an Episcopalian."

"Yes, I was confirmed at the age of eleven in St. Thomas Episcopal Church in Garrison, Maryland. My mother took me to the early communion service every Sunday morning, although she never joined the church. I haven't been back to the church since I graduated from high school, so I don't know whether or not I'm still a communicant member. According to her father, Margie is still a member of First Presbyterian Church here in Princeton. Since we've been married, we have visited many churches in the different places we've lived, but we've never joined anywhere."

"Where are you attending now?"

"During the off-season and when the Orioles are on the road, we have visited a number of different churches. But this past winter we started attending Faith Presbyterian Church, which is not far from where we live. The children enjoy going to Sunday school there too. We like the young minister—Renwick Jackson."

"Oh, yes—Ren Jackson. He's one of our graduates."

"Is that so? He's co-pastor with his uncle, Walter Jackson. I understand the older Mr. Jackson has health problems, so his nephew has been doing most of the preaching."

"Have you and your wife thought about joining Faith Presbyterian Church?"

"As a matter of fact, we have. Ever since my visit with Dr. Mackay I've been thinking about becoming a Presbyterian. There's no chance that Margie would ever want to become an Episcopalian. She has never felt comfortable in an Episcopal service. A couple of Sundays ago we signed a visitor card at Faith Church and checked a box indicating our interest, but no one has contacted us yet."

"I'm glad you've done that. You don't have to be a Presbyterian to come to Princeton, of course. We have many other denominations represented in our student body. But you and your family should have a church home."

"We realize that."

"And you'll need a letter of recommendation from a pastor. You also ought to have the endorsement of your local church. As a Presbyterian you would be taken under care of the session—that's the board of elders, the ruling body of the local congregation."

"We'll get in touch with Mr. Jackson and talk with him about it."

"Good!"

Although he obviously could make no promises at that time, I walked out of Dean Butler's study that night feeling very encouraged about my chances of being accepted at Princeton Theological Seminary.

We left Princeton late Sunday afternoon, having had a wonderful visit with Margie's parents, both of whom were now fully in favor of my going to seminary, especially if it meant our moving to Princeton. We were home by 9:30 p.m., and in five minutes the children were asleep in their beds.

Fifteen minutes later the telephone rang, and the voice on the other end of the line said, "Hello, Mr. Armstrong, this is Ren Jackson."

5

The Point of No Return

Imagine that! Having just talked about him the night before, I pick up the phone, and who should be on the line but the man we needed to see!

"I'm so glad you called, Mr. Jackson. Margie and I were talking about making an appointment to see you."

"I could come by your house tonight, if it isn't too late."

After checking with Margie, I replied, "We'd be glad to see you. Do you know where Lochwood Road is?"

"I sure do."

"Our house is No. 1536. We'll put the porch light on."

"Fine! I'll be there in a few minutes."

It was ten minutes, to be exact, when the Rev. J. Renwick Jackson Jr. appeared at our front door. He was even taller than he appeared in the pulpit. His whole face lit up when he smiled, and his sparkling eyes reflected both a lively sense of humor and a compassionate heart. We were instantly drawn to this likeable young pastor, who came into our home as a stranger and left as a friend.

We were soon on a first-name basis, as I unfolded the story of my call and all that had happened since, including my interview with Dean Butler the night before. "That's why we wanted to talk with you about joining Faith Church. We have visited your church many times, and our children have been attending Sunday school there."

"Are you still on the roll at St. Thomas?"

The Rev. J Renwick Jackson, Jr., associate pastor at Faith Presbyterian Church, where Margie and I had been worshiping. Ren became a very good friend.

"I don't know, but I'll find out."

"If so, they may be willing to give you a letter of transfer. If not, you can join on reaffirmation of faith. In your case, Margie, you could simply write for a letter of transfer, since you know that you are still a member of First Presbyterian Church."

After hearing Ren's clear answers to a number of questions, Margie and I looked at each other and said, almost simultaneously, "I think we should join Faith Church!"

"Wonderful!" exclaimed Ren, beaming from ear to ear. "I'll be in touch with you about the next new members class. We should wait until after you have announced your resignation from the Orioles, don't you think?"

I agreed. The focus of our conversation then shifted to Princeton Seminary. Ren's enthusiasm for his alma mater was completely contagious, as he regaled us with tales of his seminary experiences. I was later to discover that the exploits of Ren Jackson and his seminary cohorts were legendary, and that he was one of Dr. Mackay's "fair-haired boys."

As we were beginning to wind down, I broached the subject of my needing a letter of recommendation from my pastor. "The seminary is pushing me for one, but I'm embarrassed about asking you to write a letter, when you hardly know me. Could you write one on the basis of our conversation tonight?"

"Of course! After all, we've been talking for three hours. I feel as if I know you a lot better than I do some of the people for whom I've written letters. I'll try to get one off to Donald Butler tomorrow. I'll explain that you and Margie have been worshiping at Faith Church for several months and will be joining with the next new-members class."

Ren suggested we close with a prayer. I remember feeling a little uncomfortable as the three of us joined hands. That was something I had never done before. Even so, Margie and I were immensely impressed by our new pastor and tremendously grateful for his visit. We could hardly believe it was one o'clock in the morning when we finally said goodnight! What a weekend it had been!

The next day I sent Ren a thank-you note and enclosed a clergy pass for the 1955 season. I also telephoned the rector of St. Thomas Episcopal Church, the Rev. Dr. Philip Jensen, who, as would be expected, was surprised to hear from me. I asked if he had time to see me some day that week, and we set a date for the following day.

The lovely old church on the hill was just as I remembered it. What memories flooded my heart as I stood at the rear of the sanctuary, gazing at the steps of the chancel where I had knelt at the age of twelve to be confirmed by the bishop, and at the altar rail where I had received communion week after week. As I stood there completely absorbed in my nostalgic recollections, it was almost as if I were transported momentarily back to those halcyon days of my boyhood.

My reverie was abruptly ended by the voice of the sexton, who inquired, "May I help you?"

"I'm here to see Dr. Jensen."

I was then led to the rector's office, where Dr. Jensen was waiting for me. How good it was to see him again after so many years! He could not have been more cordial. He had been the beloved chaplain at nearby McDonogh School, where his son and I were classmates from the lower school grades through high school. He remembered that I had written him while I was overseas in the Navy during World War II.

Dr. Jensen and I had a wonderful time reminiscing about our McDonogh days, and I was amazed that he also remembered having awarded me the prize at commencement one year for submitting the best essay in the lower school on the theme "What God Means to Me." The prize was a leather-bound Bible, bearing the following inscription:

To Richard Armstrong,
for best essay in Bible examination
given to Lower School at McDonogh.

P. J. Jensen, Chaplain
June 5, 1936

St. Thomas Episcopal Church, Garrison Forest, Maryland, where I was confirmed at the age of eleven. The church was just as I remembered it as boy.

I did not confess to Dr. Jensen that the prize had been collecting dust in my bookcase for all the intervening years! After my Damascus Road experience, when we returned from Florida, I had taken it off the shelf and had been reading it most every night before going to bed. As I plowed through the King James Version, beginning at the book of Genesis, I had no confidence whatsoever that I was understanding the message. The Bible was a mystery to me at that point in my life, and my reading of it was out of a sense of obligation rather than inspiration.

When we finally got around to the purpose of my visit, Dr. Jensen's face beamed in response to the announcement of my desire to enter the ministry. "Marvelous! Marvelous!" he exclaimed. I told him that I had applied for admission to Princeton Seminary and wondered if he would be willing to write a letter in my behalf. "I guess you'd have to base it on your memories of me as a McDonogh boy."

"Why, certainly I'll write a letter for you. I've known you and your parents for twenty-five years."

"Since I've decided to study for the Presbyterian ministry, Margie and I have decided to join the Presbyterian church where we have been worshiping. I don't know if I'm still a communicant member here, but would you also be willing to write a letter commending me to Faith Presbyterian Church?"

"Of course. You know, I feel very close to the Presbyterians. Peter Marshall and I have exchanged pulpits from time to time, and I have many friends who are Presbyterian ministers. There's not that much difference in the way we do things here at St. Thomas. As you know, we're not high church."

I was sorry Margie could not have been with me to meet the towering rector of St. Thomas, who had been in the famous Canadian Black Watch Regiment in World War I. She would have been as reluctant as I to say goodbye to this wonderful man, whose influence on me had been much greater than I realized as a boy.

A few days later I received a copy of the letter that Dr. Jensen had written to Princeton Seminary, with a handwritten note informing me that he had formally commended me to the spiritual care of Faith Church.

On the third of May I also wrote to the Princeton University registrar requesting that a transcript of my academic record be sent to the seminary. With that I hoped to have fulfilled all righteousness, as far as the Princeton Seminary admissions committee was concerned. Now there was nothing more I could do but wait and hope. As anxious as I was to pass this next hurdle in the pursuit of my call, I was much too busy to be impatient about hearing from Princeton. The demands of managing the frantic activities of the Orioles public relations department left no time for thumb twiddling. The call of God was not on hold but on "call waiting," for it was constantly on the back of my mind, and it colored the way I viewed everything I was doing. My responsibilities with the ball club took on not less but greater importance, as I was more determined than ever to do the best job I could possibly do, for as long as I was there. That too was part of my calling, though I would not have put it in those terms at the time.

The waiting was made easier by a rather amusing incident that took place about two weeks later. Before every home game our public relations department was a madhouse. Our large outer office, where my associate, Bill Higdon, and our three secretaries held sway, was the center of activity, with a steady stream of people flowing in and out—fans; reporters; broadcasters; feature writers; people involved in pregame promotions or special events; visiting characters of all sorts seeking information, interviews, or whatever, and always needing whatever it was in a hurry. Through it all the telephones would be ringing incessantly, adding to the confusion. It could be an SOS from the press box or the clubhouse or the pass gate or the PA announcer or an outside call from a visiting dignitary asking for tickets, or the receptionist asking whether to admit still another visitor to the bedlam. I was used to those pregame flurries. They were part of the behind-the-scenes excitement of baseball, and the busier it got, the better I liked it. A major league publicity or public relations director has to run on a fast track.

On Saturday, May 14, the Orioles were hosting the Chicago White Sox for the final day of a three-game series. Things were as busy as ever as game time drew near. The outer office was bustling with visiting press and others. I was talking with a sportswriter in my office, when I received a call from the receptionist announcing that there was a gentleman named Jim Quay in the lobby asking to see me.

"Quay . . . Quay," I said to myself. "Who is Jim Quay? I don't know any Jim Quay . . . " Then the light dawned. It had to be Dr. Quay from Princeton Seminary! "Please show him in," I said to the receptionist. "I have someone with me at the moment, but I'll be right out."

The reporter who was with me politely excused himself, saying, "I'm all finished, Dick. Many thanks." As we walked out of my office together through the door at the opposite end of the outer office strode a tall, dignified gentleman, wearing glasses and a stiff white shirt collar with a dark suit and vest. "Dr. Quay?" I asked, extending my hand to him. As he grasped and shook my hand vigorously, he blurted out in a resonant bass voice that could have been heard by everyone in the stadium, "So you want to go into the ministry!"

For an instant I was mortified. I hoped my expression concealed my chagrin at this inopportune divulgence of my closely guarded secret. Of all places for such an unwitting revelation, uttered in innocence by a man who had no idea of the consequences of his *malapropos*—here we were in the publicity office, surrounded by representatives of the news media! I expected the reaction to be one of complete shock, followed by a bombardment of questions, "What's this about your going into the ministry?"

But there was no stunned silence, no reaction whatsoever. It was business as usual. Those newshounds, who were always so hungry for anything they could use, so quick to sniff out the slightest hint of a story, paid no attention whatsoever to the sonorous words of this dignified stranger who had wandered into their midst! The only explanation for their failure to hear Dr. Quay's inadvertent disclosure I can offer is that what he said was so totally foreign to the context in which they were operating that it sailed right over their heads. They heard the words but not the message. They were too engrossed in the business of the moment, which was baseball.

My astonishment was exceeded only by my relief as I quickly whisked my clerical visitor out the door, before he could utter another word. "Let's go sit up in the stands, where we can talk privately," I said by way of explanation for our sudden departure. The visiting White Sox were having batting practice, as we climbed to the top of the lower deck, where there was no one within two hundred feet of us. There we sat and visited for several minutes.

The vice president of Princeton Seminary was a man in his late sixties. He had been a missionary in Egypt for twenty-eight years, before returning to the United States to assume his post at Princeton Seminary. He had a delightful sense of humor, and despite my initial reaction to his well-intended but ill-timed greeting, I liked this warm-hearted man with whom I hoped to be working.

Dr. Quay explained that he and his wife were driving to Washington, DC, and he thought they should swing by Memorial Stadium in Baltimore on the chance of being able to meet me and at least say hello. From his quick glimpse at the goings-on in my office he was well aware that I was busy, and since Mrs. Quay was waiting in the car, we could not talk as long as either of us would have liked.

Speaking as if my coming to Princeton were a foregone conclusion, Dr. Quay complimented me on the public relations materials I had sent, described the nature of the work we would be doing, and outlined my duties, which sounded as if they would relate as much to fundraising as to public relations. Because of Dr. Quay's use of the conjunction *when* rather than *if,* my excitement level was rising rapidly.

As we tramped back down the stadium steps, my unexpected visitor thanked me for taking time to talk, but I assured him that it was my pleasure. And indeed it was! At the parking lot, where our polite attendants had allowed the New Jerseyans to park temporarily, I was glad to have the opportunity to meet Mrs. Quay, a very gracious, grandmotherly lady. "Ida is my chauffeur," her husband explained. "I can't drive a car anymore because of my poor eyesight."

I thanked them again for coming out of their way to see me. "I'm more enthusiastic than ever about coming to Princeton, Dr. Quay, and about being your assistant, if the seminary accepts my application."

As Mrs. Quay started to back the car out of their parking space, Dr. Quay's last words to me were, "You should be hearing soon!"

The Rev. Dr. James K. Quay, vice president of Princeton Seminary, whose unexpected drop-in visit at Memorial Stadium gave me hope that my application for admission would be accepted.

I did. The following Monday Margie called me at the office to tell me that a letter from Princeton Seminary had arrived in the morning mail. Fortunately there was no game that day so that I was able rush right home. We lived just over a mile from the stadium, and it took only a few minutes for me to drive to our house on Lochwood Road, where we eagerly opened the envelope. The letter was dated May 14, 1955, from Dr. Mackay, telling me that I had been accepted and that formal notification from Dean Butler would follow shortly.

"I am also happy to inform you," he continued in the second paragraph, "that at a meeting of a committee of the Board of Trustees, held yesterday in Philadelphia, Dr. Quay and I were authorized to employ your services to assist him in his work of promotion and public relations." He went on to suggest that I visit the campus again to discuss with him and Dr. Quay the responsibilities, remuneration, and other matters relating to my work at the seminary.

Now I knew why Dr. Quay had spoken as if the decision about my coming to Princeton was a fait accompli! With this official confirmation in hand, I could at last announce my decision to resign from the Orioles in order to study for the ministry.

There were, however, some important considerations regarding that process, such as the wording of the announcement, and decisions regarding who needed to be told personally and in what order, before I notified the press. The timing had to be just right so that the news would not leak out prematurely. There was no question that our parents should be the first to know. We agreed that Margie would call her parents right away, while I returned to the stadium to tell my dad. I was eager to show him the letter, and to ask his advice about notifying others.

My father was as excited about the letter as I was. We decided that I should make the announcement to the press on Thursday, May 19, which was another open date. That would give me time to speak in person to Clarence Miles, Paul Richards, and other persons in the Orioles front office, including those in my own department. Instead of sending out a formal press release, I would simply call the sportswriters and announcers who covered the Orioles and tell them the news over the phone. They were, after all, my friends, and they deserved to hear from me in person.

Clarence Miles was the first person on the list, since it was he who had hired me. The next morning I went to see him in his downtown office, where he greeted me very cordially. After an exchange of pleasantries, I told him that I wanted him to be the first to know of my decision to resign from the Orioles at the end of the season in order to enter Princeton Theological Seminary. *Surprised* would be much too mild a word to describe the initial reaction of the genial president of the Orioles, but then he seemed genuinely interested in knowing how I had come to that decision.

"I feel it is a call of God," I replied. "That's all I can say. It is not something I ever dreamed of doing."

Clarence nodded as if my answer had satisfied him. "I was hoping you would remain with the Orioles for many years, Dick, but you have to do what your heart tells you. I'm glad you'll be with us through the end of the season. That will give us some time to find your successor. When do you want to make the announcement?"

"Thursday, if that's all right with you. There are a few people, like Paul Richards and Art Ehlers, whom I need to tell personally, so they don't hear it from somebody else, or read about it in the newspapers. I'd appreciate your not saying anything about this before Thursday."

The visit with Clarence Miles marked the point of no return for me. I remember having the strange sensation, as I walked out of his office, of having closed the door on my baseball career, even though our move to Princeton was still a long way off and my work with the Orioles was far from over. Now that the president of the ball club had accepted my resignation, it was official—and final. I was feeling a twinge of reality.

Throughout the rest of that day I was busy having variations of that conversation with each of my front office colleagues whom I needed to see in person. The Orioles were playing at home that night, but I was able to squeeze in private visits with each of them, beginning with Paul Richards. Paul's reaction was most gracious and gratifying. I think I had risen high in his estimation on opening day, when I presented him with a fifty-foot, eight millimeter color film I had shot of him with president Eisenhower. Ike threw out the first ball. For whatever reason, Paul and I had developed a very friendly relationship, even though I had never become one of his golf-playing or socializing buddies.

Jack Dunn, Art Ehlers, and the other persons with whom I shared the news were surprised but supportive. So were the sportswriters. On Thursday, May 19, the story appeared in the Baltimore newspapers and was picked up by the wire services. It was interesting how the boys in the press box tried to explain my decision or suggest reasons of their own. My friend Hugh Trader of the *Baltimore News-Post* "quoted" me as saying, "I have felt that this is my calling for a long, long time . . . In the back of my mind I have always wanted to enter the ministry." The words he put in my mouth could not have been further from the truth, but then how could I expect the boys in the press box to understand my sense of being called, when I didn't fully understand it myself?

The news articles precipitated a wave of telephone calls and letters from friends far and near. In the conversations that ensued it was I who was often surprised by the attempts of my friends to account for my decision. It was, after all, quite unusual for a major league baseball executive to resign in order to enter the ministry. Indeed, it had never happened before, and they had a difficult time understanding why anyone would do such a thing.

"Was it because of your son?" asked my good friend Ed Pollock, sports editor of the *Philadelphia Evening Bulletin* and in my view the dean of Philadelphia sportswriters. Ed had telephoned to say that he wanted to write a column about me.

"I don't understand your question, Ed. What does my son have to do with it?" That idea had never occurred to me.

"I just thought maybe it was because your son has leukemia."

"No," I replied, still puzzled by the suggestion.

Sensing my bewilderment, Ed tactfully changed the subject. A person of high principles and, as I later learned, a man of deep faith, he and his wife, Nan, had been our good friends since our years in Philadelphia. I had always held him in high esteem. As a fair-minded and wise observer of people, Ed Pollock was one of whom it could be truthfully said, he was a credit to his profession. When his column finally appeared, it was very sensitively written, but I was amused by his conjectured attempt to explain my call. He too quoted me as saying that I had been considering the ministry for many years, as if I were somehow cut out for the ministry. That, of course, in my mind was not the case.

Ed was the first but by no means the only person to make a connection between Ricky's illness and my decision to become a minister. My brother Herb, who was living and working in France, in responding to my letter informing him of my decision, asked in his return letter: "Do you think there is any connection between Ricky's illness and your decision to become a minister?"

I was probably the last to see the connection, and I now regard that initial failure to see it as further evidence of the provi-

My brother Herb, whom I would later call a seeking agnostic, was nevertheless very interested in and supportive of my decision to enter the ministry. From the time he was a boy Herb had courted danger, so it was not surprising that he volunteered to be the test officer for the first parachute-artillery battery and later was recruited for the OSS in World War II, serving in covert missions in occupied France. He was twice interrogated and released by the Gestapo.

dential grace of God. Had I for one moment suspected that my desire to become a minister was the result of Ricky's illness, either as an attempt to bargain with God for Ricky's life or to atone for whatever I may have done to cause God's disfavor, I would still be in baseball, because I would have suspected my motives. Thus my written answer to my brother's question was as follows: "There is a connection between Ricky's illness and my entering the ministry, but I didn't realize it until long after I'd already decided to do it. Since we first learned of Ricky's disease, we have prayed that we would understand God's will and that somehow we would be better people as a result of it. Perhaps this is one of God's ways of answering that prayer."

The God who understands us better than we understand ourselves knew that I could not trust my acceptance of a call for which I had bargained. God never allowed that thought to cross my mind, *until* I was mature enough in my faith to understand how my son's illness had indeed helped make me more open and receptive to the call of God. Through the experience of Ricky's suffering Margie and I had learned some lessons about life that we might otherwise never have known. It was after being told our son had leukemia that Margie and I started praying together for the first time and attending church more regularly, all of which was part of my preparation for God's unexpected call.

The more I had to answer people's questions about my call, the clearer some things became. I was learning with the hindsight of faith how God guides, as well as provides for, those whom God calls.

In the midst of all the cards and notes from well-wishers came the formal letter of admission from Dr. Butler. My cousin Maurice was overjoyed when I telephoned to tell him about my being accepted at Princeton Seminary and to thank him again for his excellent suggestions, which had started that whole process. I had been keeping him informed about my meetings with Dr. Mackay and Dean Butler. I also wrote a long letter to Dr. Poteat in Florida, bringing him up-to-date on all that had happened.

Responding to Dr. Mackay's expressed desire for me to meet with him and with Dr. Quay to discuss the duties and terms of my employment at the seminary, I agreed to come to Princeton on May 30, when the Orioles were scheduled to play a Memorial Day doubleheader in Boston. I took Ricky with me on the train so that he could visit with his Princeton grandparents while I was meeting with Dr. Mackay and Dr. Quay. For me it was a very productive day, most of which was spent with Dr. Quay, who described in detail the various things I would be doing. The time with Dr. Mackay was much briefer but most encouraging, as he informed me what my salary would be. The figure was more than generous, although it would represent, as was to be expected, a drastic reduction in our income. Even more important was the news that we would be able to live in one of the seminary apartments for married students in North-South Hall, a large, stucco-faced building perpendicular to Stockton Street on the seminary's Tennent campus. The rent for any seminary apartment was considerably less than the going rates in Princeton.

Ricky had a wonderful time with his Grampy and Granmama, and we both had much to tell my parents, who met us at the train station that night and drove us home. Margie was thrilled when I told her about the apartment, which, though tiny, would be adequate for our needs while in seminary. Everything seemed to be working out perfectly.

In the meantime, life at the stadium was proceeding as usual, and I still had a job to do for the Orioles.

6

A Few Surprises but No Regrets

Life with the Orioles, however, was not all work and no play for the front office staff. During the off-season we would have some wild touch football games in the stadium, and during the regular season we had our own Oriole staff softball team. We played once or twice a week in a very competitive league that included teams representing the Baltimore Police Department, the Baltimore Fire Department, and the Baltimore Colts, among others. The Colts were literally and figuratively the heaviest hitters in the league, but we managed to beat them the two times we played them that summer.

Since the teams were allowed to recruit players to complete their rosters, I suggested that we invite Ren Jackson to join our Oriole team. Ren was pleased to be asked and quickly proved his worth as our smooth-fielding first baseman. During one of our games, in trying to beat out an infield grounder, I crashed into the opposing first baseman, who dropped the throw from the shortstop. As the first baseman dusted himself off, he said in a voice loud enough for everyone on the field to hear, "I can't believe that guy is gonna be a minister!"

All of a sudden my behavior was unbecoming a minister! Already I had bumped up against the double standard that all ministers have to live with. One can resent and complain about it, but one forgets it or ignores it at one's own peril.

That was a new experience for me, and unfortunately, it was not the only time it happened. An even more embarrassing incident took place a week later, while I was playing shortstop for our team. The umpiring, which was never very reliable, was particularly bad on this evening in June. After what I thought was an inexcusably atrocious call by the umpire at second base, in the heat of the moment I said some rather unflattering things under my breath about the level of that gentleman's intelligence. My comments were apparently loud enough for him to hear, for he angrily spun around to address me. I was sure he was going to say, "You're out of here!" But instead, he shook his head in obvious disbelief and blared, "A fine minister you're going to be!" That comment shut me up in a hurry!

After the game I overheard him say to the other umpire, "Now if you told me that first baseman was going to be a minister, I could believe that." Little did he know that Ren was already one!

I did apologize to the gentleman for my remarks, which in my overly competitive opinion were well deserved on his part, but in his perception were hardly appropriate on my part. After watching Jimmy Dykes and his managerial peers in action, I had looked upon vocal commentary like that simply as part of the game, but apparently such behavior was not becoming a minister. I had learned my lesson.

Not too many weeks later that lesson was reinforced, when I experienced the flipside of the double standard. I had come down to Baltimore from Princeton to attend to some personal business. While there I took advantage of the opportunity to drop in on my friends at the stadium. After making the rounds of the offices, I walked down to the clubhouse and then out onto the field, where I stopped to say hello to some of the members of the ground crew, who were getting the football field ready for the Baltimore Colts. As we were chatting, one of the men suddenly interrupted the conversation to apologize to me for the four-letter words they were using. "Excuse us, Reverend," he said in a tone of unfeigned embarrassment.

I laughed and said, "After all these years of listening to you fellows, now you apologize!"

"Yeah, but now you're a minister!" said my unerudite friend, whose Roman Catholic faith demanded respect for the clergy.

"But I'm not a minister yet. And besides, it's not the fact that a minister hears you but the fact that you said it that counts with God."

"You've got a point there, Reverend!"

I had been a seminary student for less than a month, but to these men who had once called me by my first name, I was now "Reverend" Armstrong. Not only had I to watch my language, but they had to watch their language around me! This too was part of my initiation into the realities of the double standard.

The summer of 1955 was a memorable one for me in more ways than one. I suppose it was the realization that my days in baseball were numbered that caused me to savor every one of them. In addition to performing my regular duties, I wanted to complete a number of projects and leave everything in order for the person who would succeed me as public relations director. In the precomputer age one of the most important marks of efficient office management was to be able to find what you were looking for in your files. I wanted my successor to be able to retrieve whatever information was needed whenever it was needed.

Mr. Miles had immediately been swamped with applications for the position I was vacating, all of which he turned over to me with the request that I submit my recommendations to the board of directors regarding the staffing of the public relations department. In response I drafted a lengthy report describing the functions and outlining all the responsibilities of the department, and suggesting various staffing possibilities. I had no desire or intention to choose my successor, but I was happy to spell out some viable options.

Despite my growing anticipation of our move to Princeton, the days flew by. So did the nights, whether or not the team was home, because there was much to be done at home on the "off" nights. Having engaged a real estate agent and put our house up for sale, we had many fix-up and clean-up projects in order to prepare for potential buyers. We had chosen the property on Lochwood Road partly because of its resale value. Never did we dream that it would be on the market even longer than our home in Havertown.

Soon after receiving Dean Butler's letter of admission, I had started poring over the Princeton Seminary catalogue. Reading the course descriptions was both fascinating and frightening, as I realized how unprepared I was for the kind of subjects I would be studying. My background in economics and business administration hardly fitted me for a theological education. I was thoroughly intrigued, however, by the whole new world of study into which I would be diving headlong in the fall. The language requirements, of which I had already been made aware by Dean Butler, were for me the only intimidating aspect of the curriculum.

I did not relish the thought of having to study Greek and Hebrew, but I decided to get a running start on at least one of the language requirements.

Having been advised by Ren Jackson to take the Greek course during my first year, I inquired of him the name of the text that I would be using and ordered a copy of J. Gresham Machen's *New Testament Greek for Beginners*. The book was then in its twenty-sixth printing and had been used by an entire generation of Princeton Seminary students. By the time we moved to Princeton I had worked through the first ten chapters. That proved to be one of the best academic decisions I have ever made, for it enabled me to stay ahead of the daily assignments and to sail through the yearlong Greek course with ease. Not only that but I loved it!

Ren also gave me a Revised Standard Version of the Bible, which he said would be easier reading, and suggested that I start with the New Testament. That proved to be a helpful suggestion, although I must admit that I continued to look upon the Bible as a book of religious myths and ancient stories from which believers could derive meaning and inspiration. I was forcing myself to believe it was somehow God's word, but there were lingering doubts about the parts that strained my intellectual credulity. How was I to understand what my mind could not accept as literally true? I had so much to learn!

Throughout the summer weeks Margie's and my dominant concern had always been our son Ricky, whose first remission had ended shortly after we returned from spring training. Since then he had been through progressively shorter periods of remission. In between his pseudo-euphoric periods of temporary recovery would be days of terrible suffering, usually involving hospitalization, blood transfusions, and painful treatments. In order to be home as much as I could be at night during these difficult times, I had been accepting as few speaking engagements as possible.

It was difficult to refuse my friend Charlie Plitt, however, whose persistence finally prevailed upon me to speak to his service club. Charlie and I had played against and with each other in high school and sandlot baseball, and he wanted me to talk about how I had decided to become a minister. Because of our friendship and his interest in my call, I accepted his invitation.

That engagement was one I shall never forget, not just because it was the first time I had spoken publicly about my call, but because of what happened to me while I was speaking. Near the end of my talk I explained that at first I had hesitated to accept Charlie's invitation to speak, because of my son's illness and the fact that I was needed at home. As I began to describe what Ricky was going through at that time, the full impact of the situation suddenly swept over me and I could not continue speaking.

That was the first time I had ever "choked up" in the midst of a speech, and I was terribly embarrassed. There was a long, awkward silence, as I struggled to regain my composure. When I was finally able to speak, I apologized to the club members and quickly concluded my remarks. Rough-hewn but warmhearted, my friend thanked me with tears in his eyes. "Please don't apologize for your tears, Dick," he said to me. "They meant as much to me as anything else you said."

Charlie Plitt's kind words did not erase my embarrassment, but they did teach me that God can use even what we think are our failures to touch people's hearts.

While all these things were happening, the most important event for Margie and me in the summer of 1955 occurred on June 6, when we were received into the membership of Faith Presbyterian Church. Ren Jackson had told us that would be our first opportunity after the news of my resignation from the Orioles had been made public. I met with the session that Monday night and shared with the elders all that had been happening in our lives. I also explained that Margie could not appear with me, as she was needed at home. Since she was joining by letter of transfer and because Ren had met with us on more than one occasion, the session was happy to receive her in absentia.

At Ren's recommendation the session also voted to take me under their care as a candidate for the ministry. That was a necessary first step toward my later being taken under care of the Baltimore Presbytery. I had learned about this process from Marcus Priester.

Ren Jackson's warm welcome and introduction that night made me feel very much at ease. The older Mr. Jackson was also there and seemed to be a very caring man. He was having great difficulty speaking, so Ren moderated the meeting. He maintained his usual pleasant demeanor as he led the session through the formalities of examining and receiving me into the membership of Faith Presbyterian Church. As we exchanged glances once or twice, I suspected that he knew I was thinking of the incongruity of his decorum as moderator and his uninhibited enjoyment of the late-night jam sessions in our family room. Ren's free spirit was a refreshing contradiction of the stereotypical image of ecclesiastical stuffiness. We had become good friends.

Faith Presbyterian Church, Baltimore, Maryland, where Margie and I had been worshiping and where our children were attending Sunday school.

One does not always realize how many friends and well-wishers one has until there is some major event in one's life. Margie and I kept receiving letters and telephone calls from people who had read about my going into the ministry. In many of the letters there were often words of praise for the great "sacrifice" we were making in order to go to seminary. The truth is that neither Margie nor I ever thought for one second that we were making any kind of financial sacrifice. Our well-intentioned friends were invariably thinking about our giving up the glamour and material benefits of a career in baseball. Although we wondered at first how we would support ourselves while I was in seminary, we had absolutely no regrets about our change of course, nor did we consider that there was anything virtuous about our resulting lower income status. To our friends my leaving baseball was a sacrifice, but not to us. Their compliments were totally undeserved.

Whatever sadness I felt about leaving baseball had to do not with its material benefits but with the severing of ties with the game I had loved all my life and the friends I had made along the way. I was haunted by John Bodo's gloomy prediction that the "Rev." in front of my name would mean the end of my close relationship with sports, which next to my family had always been my first love. Anyone who loves sports can understand that feeling.

Perhaps I would have looked upon the permanent closing of that door as a sacrifice, had something not happened to remind me once again so potently that one can never outgive God.

7

What Sacrifice?

It began with a long-distance telephone call one morning in July. The man on the other end of the line identified himself as Don McClanen, from Norman, Oklahoma. He said he had read about my going into the ministry and asked if he could make an appointment to see me. "I'm visiting my parents outside of Philadelphia, and I was wondering if I could come down to see you tomorrow. I've been contacting people in sports who are Christians. I'd like to talk with you about a Christian athletes organization which I'm trying to get started."

I was immediately intrigued. We made a date for the following morning, and about 11:00 a.m. a nice-looking, amiable young man was ushered into my office. "I'm Don McClanen," he said, extending his hand. We visited for about an hour, during which time I learned that he had just recently resigned as basketball coach at Eastern Oklahoma A&M in order to devote himself full time to an organization called the Fellowship of Christian Athletes (FCA). With the encouragement of Branch Rickey, then general manager of the Pittsburgh Pirates, and the financial support of a number of Pittsburgh businessmen and others who were excited by his vision, Don had been able to pursue the dream that had germinated while he was a student at Oklahoma A&M, now called Oklahoma State University. The idea of starting an organization of Christian athletes and coaches had come to him when he was preparing a three-minute testimony that he had been asked to give in his church on the topic "Making My Vocation Christian."

What Sacrifice?

At noon I drove Don to our house, where Margie was expecting us for lunch. Our conversation continued at the table for two more hours, during which Don told us the reactions of the nineteen sports personalities he had written about his idea. Branch Rickey was one of fourteen who had said they were interested and would help. The list included such well-known athletes as "Deacon" Dan Towler of the Los Angeles Rams, Brooklyn Dodgers pitcher Carl Erskine, Olympic gold medalist pole-vaulter Bob Richards, and Cleveland Browns quarterback Otto Graham.

Don had also very wisely sought the advice and support of several ministers, including a prominent Presbyterian preacher, the Rev. Louis H. Evans Sr., who responded enthusiastically to the idea but encouraged Don to make sure his dream was not duplicating some other ministry. It was not. The Rev. James D. Stoner, then director of University Christian Mission for the National Council of Churches, saw the potential of the FCA as a powerful influence on college campuses and became personally involved. The Rev. Roe H. Johnston, former Navy all-American end, who was then pastor of the First Presbyterian Church of Indianapolis, enthusiastically paved the way for a major foundation grant. All of these men served on the FCA's first advisory board, of which Roe Johnston was to become the first president.

The newly formed organization had been granted a charter in the state of Oklahoma in November 1954. In the summer of 1955 the young founder became its first executive director, when he opened a small office in the back of the First National Bank Building in Norman, Oklahoma. The FCA was now officially launched.

Sharing a love of sports and having had the similar experience of being called by God into full-time Christian service, Don and I found we had much in common. He too was a Presbyterian, a World War II veteran, and about my age. The more we talked, the more excited we both became about how my experience in public relations and publicity could be helpful in promoting this brand-new and utterly unique movement. Don's strong faith and deep commitment were an inspiration to me, and I sensed that here was a man I would come to know and love as a Christian brother. At Don's suggestion the three of us had a closing prayer together. Unlike my first experience with Ren Jackson, this time it seemed perfectly natural to join hands across the table, and for the first time in my life I prayed aloud with someone other than my family.

I drove Don to Union Station, and as I watched him board the train for Philadelphia, I remember feeling a surge of elation, for I suddenly realized that not only could I still have a relationship with sports but that the relationship would now have a Christian focus and purpose. This was not something for which I had prayed. On the contrary, I had been quite resigned to the thought that in becoming a minister I would be closing the sports door behind me.

Now God had graciously given me something of far more value than what I had thought I was giving up. Having worked in baseball for the better part of nine years, I was well aware of the spiritual void in professional sports and of the need for the kind of witness Don hoped to facilitate through the Fellowship of Christian Athletes. What a wonderful way to relate my love of sports to my new calling!

That was my introduction to and the beginning of my involvement in the FCA, as the movement soon came to be popularly known. In spite of my enthusiasm about the concept and my desire to be helpful, little did I realize then how large a part of my life would be devoted to that ministry, and how deeply involved I would be in the formative stages of the movement and beyond. The coaches, athletes, ministers, and others I met and worked with in the FCA over the years became and have remained some of my closest friends. As has often been said by those of us in the Fellowship, our love of sports brought us together, and our love of Christ keeps us together.

So now I understand that I did not have to give up my association with sports after all. I left a career in baseball but not my association with athletics. My relationship with the world of athletics has continued to this day, as I am a trustee emeritus of the FCA's national board. Where, then, was the sacrifice in my accepting the call of God to study for the ministry? It was not the material benefits I had enjoyed in baseball, nor, as it turned out, my lifelong association with sports. I was so convinced of the reality of God's call and so excited and happy about going to seminary that I was always quick to assure my friends there was nothing at all sacrificial about my decision.

August 1961, Estes Park, Colorado. FCA founder and executive director Don McClanen and I became the best of friends. Every summer for many years our family participated in the National FCA Conferences held at the YMCA Camp near Estes Park.

What Sacrifice?

To be sure, I have sometimes had twinges of nostalgia as I've remembered my days in baseball, and there is much I still miss about my former career. But I have never felt as if leaving that career was a sacrificial move.

August 1961, Estes park, Colorado. The then-current four officers of the FCA national board of directors (L to R): Denver University athletic director Tad Wieman, president; Kansas University basketball coach Dick Harp, secretary; LSU football coach Paul Dietzel, vice president; and yours truly, treasurer, are standing near the YMCA's main auditorium. The board had lengthy meetings in those days as we adopted a constitution and mapped out plans for the fledging organization, which in a few years would become a worldwide fellowship of Christian high school, college, and professional male and female athletes, coaches, and supporters.

Estes Park FCA conference, August 1964. Princeton's all American basketball star Bill Bradley shows some admiring athletes and coaches how he does it. Many were predicting way back then that this handsome young scholar-athlete would be a national political leader someday. They were right!

The widely-viewed snapshot taken at an early FCA conference illustrates what the Fellowship is all about. *Sports Illustrated* called it "hero worship harnessed." The athletes have had their quiet time and are now studying the Bible with their conference teammates.

Not until I had been studying at Princeton Seminary for a while did I finally realize that my becoming a minister did indeed involve my giving up

May 21, 1979, FCA national headquarters, Kansas City, Missouri. I took this photo shortly before the dedication of the FCA's new national headquarters. Part of the Kansas City Sports Complex is visible in the background, the KC Royals' stadium on the left and the KC Chiefs' on the right. The FCA complex has been vastly expanded and is now their very impressive world headquarters.

June 1, 1975. Having Christian friends like former Brooklyn Dodgers pitcher Carl Erskine and Dallas Cowboys coach Tom Landry erased any regrets I had about leaving professional baseball. We were participating in the dedication of the FCA's National Resource Center near Turkey Run State Park in Indiana.

something I had not appreciated as important until I no longer had it. It was the feeling of expertise I had acquired in my previous profession. I had felt as if I knew as much about sports publicity and public relations as anyone else in the world, and I was confident and competent in my role. After sitting at the feet of my learned professors and being exposed to their broad knowledge, the variety and breadth of courses in the theological curriculum, and the vast amount of literature in the seminary's excellent library, I recognized that as an ordained minister I would never again have the kind of self-confidence I had in baseball. There would always be people who knew more than I.

Not everyone who wrote or telephoned after reading or hearing about my call looked upon it as a sacrifice. Some shared the fact they too had at one time considered the ministry. It was interesting to discover that so many people who had never mentioned their faith or indicated their church membership now were identifying themselves as members of churches. I was also surprised and pleased to receive many beautiful letters from my Jewish friends, who seemed genuinely moved by my decision.

There were some amusing incidents as well. One such incident occurred soon after the visit from Don McClanen. Mickey McConnell, who had been chief scout for the Brooklyn Dodgers under Branch Rickey, and whom I had known since my days with the Philadelphia Athletics, stopped in to see me before one of the Orioles' home games. He congratulated me on my call and completely surprised me by indicating that he too was a Presbyterian and an elder in his church.

"I never knew that, Mickey. Because of your name I always thought you were a Roman Catholic."

"That's interesting, Dick. I had always thought you were a Roman Catholic too because you worked for the Mack family!"

Mickey was then employed by the United States Rubber Corporation as director of training for Little League Baseball. He wrote the excellent training manual for Little League coaches. He told me about his association with the Yokefellow Institute, and about the fascinating work he had been doing to improve conditions for migrant farm workers. From that day on what had been a casual acquaintance developed into a strong and lasting friendship.

Throughout July and August my work with the Orioles continued to have a twin focus, as I was both keeping up and winding down. There were the usual press and fan publications to produce, including a revised edition of the *Baltimore Orioles Sketchbook,* and the daily statistical information to compile for the press. How primitive the latter process was compared to the computerized data processing available to today's statisticians! The new technologies have revolutionized the task, skills, and scope of professional sports publicity.

There were also the promotional events and all the public relations activities related to each one. There were special promotions of various proportions planned for every home game, up to and including the season's final series with the Washington Senators, September 16, 17, and 18. The opening doubleheader of that series was listed on the special-events calendar as "Firemen's Oriole Appreciation Night," sponsored by the firefighters of metropolitan Baltimore. Some top-flight entertainment had been planned for between games of the twi-night twin bill.

September 16, 1955, "Dick Armstrong Night" at Memorial Stadium. Never did I dream anything like this would ever happen to me!

Imagine my surprise when I was informed that the firemen were going to call it "Dick Armstrong Night"! I had planned and promoted many a "night" for players and others, but I never dreamed anyone would ever do that for me. This was one event for which I had very little to do with the planning!

8

Winding Down and Gearing Up

There was plenty else to do that month, as the Orioles began their final and longest homestand on September 2, 1955. Since the regular season would not end until Sunday, September 25, Margie and I realized we would have to move to Princeton before the first of September. Accordingly we made arrangements to move on Wednesday, August 31, a decision which accelerated our packing effort to a frantic pace. We had been hoping our house would be sold by then, but such was not to be the case.

In addition to the usual demands of moving, we had the problem of deciding how much of the contents of a fairly large house we could cram into a small apartment and what to do with the rest. We decided to put our unused furniture into storage in Princeton, and, because the cost was considerably less, to have our unneeded carpets cleaned and stored in Baltimore.

The house itself was in excellent condition, since we had made a number of improvements in the time we had lived there. Our front-porch awning, which had been demolished during a sudden, violent storm in mid-August, had been replaced. Upon the advice of our real estate agent, we were asking what we thought was a very reasonable price, and we could not understand, despite reports of a soft market, why we had not had any offers. We dreaded the thought of having to continue our monthly mortgage payments on our soon-to-be severely reduced income.

While readying our Lochwood Road house for sale, we were also wondering about preparing our South Hall apartment for occupancy. The seminary had a policy of providing their tenants with paint if the occupants would do the painting. The choice of colors was limited to pale green or "seminary gray," which some of the students suspected may have had theological significance. Wanting, nevertheless, to avail ourselves of the paint deal before moving in, we loaded our children and as many vital items as we could cram into our car, and headed for Princeton late Friday afternoon, August 19, 1955, arriving at 106 Broadmead early that evening.

Except for church on Sunday morning, the rest of the weekend was spent painting the apartment. Margie's mother questioned the appropriateness of our working on Sunday afternoon. That was a new thought for me, for whom Sunday had long been just another working day during the baseball season. I pointed out to her that I was used to seeing many clerical collars at the ballpark on Sunday afternoons. That argument did not impress my mother-in-law one bit.

Right or wrong, we managed to paint the entire apartment before returning to Baltimore. Although Ricky had not been feeling very well that weekend, he was thrilled to be able to help with the task. His sister Ellen and younger brother Andy had stayed with their grandmother. Sitting on a footstool, Ricky carefully guided his brush along the baseboard and as high as his aching arm could reach. The little clucking sound he made with his tongue whenever he was engaged in an activity he liked was the clue that the joy of the experience was overcoming the pain of his disease. I could not believe that a loving, compassionate God would consider sinful the sheer delight of sharing that experience with our little boy.

Although Ricky's remissions were shorter now, whatever worry we might have had about the adverse effects our moving to Princeton could possibly have on him were completely dispelled by that weekend experience, and by the enthusiasm with which all three of our children were anticipating the move as the time drew near.

Somehow we managed to be ready when the large moving van pulled up in front of our house early in the morning on Wednesday, August 31. We had labeled everything so that the movers would know what went where and could load things accordingly. Even so, it was late in the afternoon when they finally finished and left. As the rooms were emptied one by one, we were cleaning and dusting so that by the time the huge truck eased away from the curb and rumbled slowly down our narrow one-way street and out of sight, we had only a little last-minute tidying up to do.

About that time our real estate agent came by to pick up our house keys as requested. Together we made one last inspection, room by room. He was pleased with and we were proud of the way the house looked. After bidding a sad farewell to this home from which we would take away so many precious memories, and having packed our car with another load of our more-fragile possessions, our weary little family took off for Princeton.

The next morning Margie and I were waiting at the entryway to our South Hall apartment, when the moving van arrived. Because we had carefully measured and planned where everything would go, and because there was less space to be filled, the movers were finished their work in shorter time than expected. By mid-afternoon we were well settled in the cozy apartment that was to be our home for the next three years.

I returned to Baltimore by train that evening and for the next two and a half weeks was dividing my time unequally between Baltimore and Princeton. With the full knowledge and approval of Clarence Miles and Paul Richards, I turned over my publicity responsibilities to my assistant, Bill Higdon, and my promotional duties to my father, so that I could

The entryway to our apartment in South Hall, which together with North Hall (the other end of the same building) was later renamed Roberts Hall.

spend more time in Princeton and get acclimated to my new work at the seminary before classes began. Dr. Quay was eager for me to begin and wasted no time delineating my duties and involving me in various development projects. One of my immediate responsibilities was to edit *The Spire,* the seminary's external house organ.

For sentimental and other obvious reasons I wanted to be in Baltimore for the final series with the Washington Senators. Margie and the children drove down to Baltimore with me so that Margie, Ellen, and Ricky could be there for my "night" on Friday, September 16, while my two aunts were babysitting Andy. The between-games ceremony turned out to be a very nice affair, during which I had an opportunity to express my appreciation publicly to the fans and the ball club, as well as to the firefighters for sponsoring the night. They gave me some useful gifts and made me honorary assistant chief of the Baltimore Fire Department.

What a contrast between all that hoopla and the sedate atmosphere of the orientation for incoming students at Princeton Theological Seminary one week later! We had returned to Princeton after the last game, since I had said my final goodbyes to my friends in the press box, the clubhouse, and the front office. Next to my father, Jack Dunn had been the most visibly moved by the parting. I was pleased to learn that Jack was to be named assistant general manager, a title that recognized what his actual role had been.

Although I was now fully immersed in my new responsibilities in the seminary's development office, there continued to be considerable correspondence relating to the Orioles, as well as personal mail forwarded from Baltimore. Among the letters was one from, of all people, the Rev. Elmer L. Kimmell, who had been chaplain aboard the *USS Chandeleur*, informing me that he had been called to the Wilson Memorial Methodist Church of Baltimore, two blocks from my parents' home! My aunts Nora and Edith Stoll were members of his congregation. It is indeed a small world!

But that's not all. "Kim" went on to say that he had been calling on some of Wilson Memorial's inactive members who had moved out of the neighborhood. While visiting in one of the homes, he discovered that the Mr. Dunn he was calling upon was none other than the Jack Dunn of the Orioles!

Keeping up with such correspondence, while familiarizing myself with my responsibilities as assistant to Vice President Quay and preparing for my first semester of classes, kept me busy night and day. Dr. Quay was most considerate of and sympathetic to my obligations as a student and insisted that I attend the two-day orientation program. He was well aware of the fact that I was spending many nighttime hours in the office, and therefore he never objected to my having to be away from my desk in order to attend to personal or family needs. Once I knew what my class schedule would be, we established definite hours when I would be on the job. The truth of the matter is that I was putting in far more than the twenty hours a week a student was permitted to be gainfully employed. I was more like a full-time employee, and I figured nobody would mind, as long as I kept up with my studies. Whether or not I could remained to be seen.

The one problem with my working such long hours was that for the week prior to classes I was not as available to my family as I needed to be. Margie's mother kindly offered to keep Ellen and Andy for a few days so that Margie could devote her time entirely to caring for Ricky, who was in one of his low periods.

On Monday evening, September 26, the day before the opening convocation at the seminary, Clarence Miles was hosting a dinner in Baltimore for the local sportswriters and broadcasters, members of the Orioles board of directors and front office staff, the coaches, and some of the fans and local dignitaries. Mr. Miles had consulted with me about the date, to make sure Margie and I could attend, as I was to be the guest of honor. Having already had a "night" at the stadium, I was all the more flabbergasted by this additional tribute.

When the big day arrived, I put on my best dark suit, kissed Margie and Ricky goodbye, and headed out the door and down the steps. Margie felt she needed to remain at home with Ricky, who had been feeling especially miserable for the past three days. He was now under the care of Dr. Jeanette Munro, the same Princeton pediatrician who had taken care of Margie and her sisters when they were children! We were very pleased with the medical attention Ricky was receiving. He had already been to the Princeton Hospital a couple times for blood transfusions, but Dr. Munro felt that it would be better for him to be at home with us, and so did we.

I had allowed myself just enough time for the fifteen-minute walk to the Princeton Station, where I would board the "dinky" that would take me to Princeton Junction in time to catch a mid-afternoon train to Baltimore. I had given much thought to what I would say that night when I was called upon for remarks, and needless to say, I was looking forward excitedly to my very first testimonial dinner.

Margie was still waving goodbye to me when something amazing happened.

9

Heartrending News

I had gone only about ten steps when suddenly and unexpectedly the feeling came over me that I should not go to Baltimore. It was as if something or someone had stopped me in my tracks. There was no hesitation on my part whatsoever. I knew exactly what I must do. I turned and walked back toward Margie. As I mounted the steps, she looked puzzled. "Did you forget something?"

"No . . ."

Margie could tell there was something troubling me. She was caught between her inability to read my bewildered expression and her concern that I had a train to catch. "You'd better hurry. You'll miss the dinky."

"I'm not going to Baltimore."

Margie seemed relieved. She did not question my decision but accepted it as if it was the perfectly logical thing for me to do. That too was remarkable.

We went inside the apartment and closed the door. After a long, silent hug, Margie looked at me as if waiting for an explanation yet anticipating what I was going to say. "I have the strong feeling that God wants me to stay here with you. I think you need me here at home more than they need me in Baltimore. I'll call Dad and ask him to make my apologies to Mr. Miles and the others."

Margie quietly concurred. She had had so little sleep the last three days, having borne most of the burden of caring for Ricky, whose pain and general malaise had kept him awake throughout much of each of the past few nights.

Even though I was convinced that my last-minute change of plans was absolutely right, I dreaded calling my father to tell him that I was not coming down for the dinner. Dad had a strong sense of duty, which he had imparted to me as a boy. Social obligations and personal commitments were extremely important to him and to me, and I was sure he would be upset. After all, I was the guest of honor. How could I decide not to attend my own testimonial dinner, especially considering that it was Clarence Miles who was hosting it, and considering that the date had been chosen partly for my convenience? Moreover, Princeton was less than two-and-a-half hours by train from Baltimore. I could return to Princeton that same night if necessary, instead of staying over in Baltimore as I had planned to do.

There was every reason for my going to the dinner, and no obvious reason for choosing not to. Margie had already resigned herself to another sleepless night, and Ricky seemed to be holding his own, despite his discomfort. I could almost hear Dad saying, "You have to be here, Dick. You're the guest of honor. You can take a train home right after the dinner, if you feel you have to."

Once again I had completely misjudged my father's reaction. When I reached him by telephone at the stadium, I told him that I felt I was needed at home and that I could not come to the dinner. "I was all set to come, Dad, and had started out the door, but at the last minute, I suddenly realized that this is where I should be. Margie is exhausted, and I need to be here to help with Ricky, who hasn't been feeling too well."

"I understand, Dick. By all means, you stay there with Margie. I'll explain the situation to Mr. Miles and make your apologies to those present. I'm sure they'll miss you, but we'll have a good time. I'll tell you all about it."

My father, bless his heart, said exactly what I needed to hear. Whatever guilt I may have felt for reneging on the dinner was completely dispelled by his sensitive response.

Ricky was as pleased as Margie that I had decided to stay home. He and I had a very special relationship, and I cherished every minute I was able to spend with him, as well as with our other two children. We had always been extremely close as a family, but Ricky's illness had drawn us all even closer together. For sixteen months his leukemia had been a dominating reality with which each one of us had to come to grips in her or his own way. Margie and I had conscientiously and consistently tried to make sure that Ellen and Andy received their fair share of our attention, and to help them understand and not be jealous when Ricky's health problems demanded more of our time.

Those problems began in April of 1954, when all three of the children came down with the chicken pox in rapid succession: first Ellen, then Andy the next day, then Ricky two days after Andy. Andy's was the mildest case, while Ellen's was more severe. Ricky's was the worst of all, as he was covered from head to toe with terrible sores. They were even in his ears and on his tongue, and the poor little fellow was utterly miserable. All of the children had been having their normal ups and downs before that, and we and the children's doctor in Yuma, Arizona, where the Orioles had trained that year, assumed that Ricky's frequent low-grade fevers were associated with his chronic ear problems. We returned from Arizona on March 28, and six days later had received a firm offer and deposit on our Linden Drive house. Oh, what a relief it was to see the "Sold" sign on our front lawn after so many months! That was a huge worry off my mind, as I returned to Baltimore and plunged back into the mad scramble to be ready for the widely heralded inauguration of the major league Orioles. On April 15 Margie came down by train for the big parade, the special luncheon at the Park Plaza Hotel, and the opening game at Memorial Stadium. It was a long day for Margie, who did not arrive home until 12:30 a.m., but a welcome change of pace from the drudgery of caring for the house and three small children.

It was two days later that Ellen got the chicken pox, followed quickly by the other two children. Now Margie was a full-time nurse as well as housekeeper, chief cook, and bottle washer. When Ricky's temperature soared to 105 degrees, Margie called Dr. Harold Medoff at home. Dr. Medoff arrived thirty minutes later, and after examining Ricky, concluded that the high fever was due entirely to the chicken pox, the worst case he had ever seen. When I arrived from Baltimore that Friday evening, I was shocked by what I saw. Margie was completely drained from nursing three sick children, one of whom was frightfully

March 15, 1954. Ricky, wearing my cap sideways so he can see, is in front of the motel where we are staying during the Orioles' spring training in Yuma, Arizona.

limp and white as a sheet. Since the Orioles were on the road, I remained in Havertown over the weekend and helped Margie with many necessary chores around the house and with the children. We were very worried about Ricky, whose temperature remained above 104 degrees. He was delirious Saturday night. Dr. Medoff came to see him again the next day, and by Sunday evening Ricky was feeling much better.

I drove back to Baltimore early Monday morning, April 26, and that evening Ricky complained of an ear ache. Harold Medoff, who had asked to be kept informed of Ricky's condition, once again came right over. The medicine he gave Ricky apparently did the trick, because Ricky was feeling better the next day, and by Thursday, was well enough for Margie to feel safe in leaving him and the other two children with a reliable babysitter the next day, while she came down to Baltimore to go house hunting with me.

Ever since we sold our home at 2440 Linden Drive I had been scouting houses in Baltimore and had narrowed the selection to a half dozen of the most likely possibilities, one of which I was hoping Margie would choose. She did, without any prompting from me, and that very afternoon we were able to close on the property at 1536 Lochwood Road. We drove back to Havertown that same night, arriving after one o'clock in the morning. I spent the day at Connie Mack Stadium, where the Orioles were playing the Athletics in an afternoon game. It was good to see many friends of former days there.

Sunday night Ruth and Ed Emack hosted a Suburban Squires farewell party for Margie and me. Though the evening was filled with singing and laughter, we were sad to part with these musical friends with whom we had shared so many good times. I left early the next morning for Baltimore, leaving Margie to cope with the realities of our impending move. For the next two weeks, while I was in Baltimore, Margie was busy packing and trying to keep up with all her other chores. Her only relaxation was watching the Senator McCarthy hearings on television. Monday, May 10, was a low point for her, as all three children became sick at the same time. Once again it was Dr. Medoff to the rescue.

On Saturday, May 15, Margie came down to Baltimore to have lunch with two of her Wellesley classmates and to visit my mother, who had been in the hospital again for several days. The following Thursday afternoon we had settlement on the sale of our house, and I remained in Havertown to pack for three days and four nights. On Saturday Margie took Ricky to Dr. Medoff for a checkup. I returned to Baltimore on Monday morning, was in

Havertown again on Tuesday night, and back in Baltimore on Wednesday morning, tending to various matters pertaining to our impending move.

In the meantime, Ricky was continuing to see Dr. Medoff, who was concerned about Ricky's pale color, low-grade fever, and lethargic behavior. Dr. Medoff suggested it might be pernicious anemia, and ordered some blood work to be done on Sunday, May 30. When Ricky's temperature rose above 102 degrees on Monday evening, Dr. Medoff had him admitted to the University of Pennsylvania Hospital the next morning, June 1, the day before the movers were to arrive. My cousin Maurice Armstrong's wife, Irene, kindly agreed to keep Ellen, and Ruth Emack and Leo Knetzger, another good friend of many years, divided the responsibility of caring for Andy, while Margie spent the day at the hospital with Ricky.

Throughout these anxious hours Margie and I had been talking frequently on the telephone, but because the Orioles were at home, I was not able to leave Baltimore until that Tuesday night. As soon as the game ended, my father drove me to the train station and I was in Havertown by 1:00 a.m. The movers arrived the next morning on schedule, and while I scurried around after them, Margie paid another visit to Ricky in the hospital, then returned to have lunch with Ellen, Andy, and me.

By 5:00 p.m. the truck was loaded and on its way to Baltimore. Margie and I then dropped Ellen and Andy off at the Emacks' and drove down to the hospital to see Ricky. Although he was obviously not feeling well, he was in good spirits and accepted our explanation of why it was necessary for him to be where he was. He understood that the doctors were trying to find out why he had not been feeling well so that they could make him well. Saying goodbye to Ricky that afternoon was probably harder for Margie and me than for Ricky, although we tried not to show it. We explained that we had to return to the house to clean up after the movers, and that I had to go back to Baltimore in order to be there when they arrived the next morning.

Our house on Linden Drive was the first home we had ever owned, and we loved it. As happy as we had been to find a buyer, it was not without a feeling of sadness that we closed the front door for the last time, having finished our cleaning work at 9:30 p.m. Margie drove me to the Thirtieth Street station in Philadelphia, and then returned to spend the night, with Ellen and Andy, at the Emacks'.

I had borrowed the "club car" and was ready and waiting at 1536 Lochwood Road when the moving van arrived the next morning. Before anything was unloaded, I asked the three men to walk with me through the house, as I tried to tell them in a general way what items of furniture went in each room. I explained that my wife had been unavoidably detained in Philadelphia and that unfortunately I could not stay and show them where things went. "If you can't figure out where to put something, use your best judgment. If it looks as if it belongs in a bedroom, put it one of the bedrooms. Most of the boxes are marked, so just stack them up in whatever room they're marked for. I'll be back at lunchtime to see how you're getting along."

With that I left! Anyone who has ever dealt with movers may find that hard to believe, but that is exactly what I did. There were a number of things going on at the office that morning and I was totally swamped. As much as I hated not to be there with the movers, I felt I had no alternative.

Unbeknownst to me, one of my McDonogh teammates and best friends, Johnny Myers, had known we were moving that day and had stopped by the house to welcome us. At the start of the season I had pressed Johnny into service to be the first "Mr. Oriole," because, as I jokingly put it, "Johnny's legs were perfect for the part!"

I hired my friend Johnny Myers to be the first "Mr. Oriole," because as I jokingly put it, his legs were perfect for the part. The fans were amazed and would cheer with delight when Mr. Oriole would play his trumpet!

An all-around athlete who played three varsity sports, Johnny Myers was one of the most popular cadets at McDonogh. Memorial Stadium fans never got to see his face.

The giant Oriole costume was made in Baltimore by a young man named Tinker, whose famous relative was the Chicago Cubs shortstop of the celebrated Tinker-to-Evers-to-Chance double-play combination. Created in 1954, our Mr. Oriole was, to my knowledge, the first such stylized mascot in major league baseball, and Johnny Myers gave the jaunty bird its distinctive personality. A creative artist and an accomplished jazz musician, Johnny was one of the most talented people I have ever known. With Johnny Myers inside, Mr. Oriole was the only trumpet-playing bird in captivity!

When the movers told him about my having to leave them on their own, Johnny immediately took charge and supervised the whole operation. Later that morning my father drove me back to the house. We were both dreading what it might look like without my having been there to direct traffic. But instead of chaos, we found Johnny Myers hard at work, and I was amazed at how accurately he had directed the placement of the main pieces of furniture. There were a few things that had to be shifted around, but the relocating was easily accomplished.

Johnny and I stayed until the men finished unloading the truck by mid-afternoon, and then my friend drove me back to the stadium. I had just walked in to my office, when my Dad appeared at the door. "Could I see you a minute, Dick? Let's go over to my office."

I could see that my father wanted to talk privately, and since there several people in my office at the time, including Johnny Myers, we walked down the hall to his. Dad seemed very upset about something. He closed the door behind him and before either of us had sat down, he turned toward me and said, hesitatingly, "I don't know how to tell you this, Dick. I'm afraid I have bad news for you . . ."

An instant sense of dread swept over me, as I waited for my father to tell me what I had to know but did not want to hear. There was a sick, sinking feeling in the pit of my stomach, the oppressive weight of anxiety about an announced but unknown tragedy. "What is it, Dad? Tell me . . ."

"It's about Ricky. Dr. Medoff called a few minutes ago. Ricky has leukemia . . . I'm so sorry, Dick . . ."

For a moment I was stunned. "Oh, dear God! I never dreamed it could be something like that. Are they sure it's leukemia?"

"According to the blood tests . . ."

"How serious is it, Dad? What did Dr. Medoff say?"

"I'm afraid it's very serious, Dick."

"Is there any hope of a cure?"

"There's always hope. But it looks pretty bad right now. I asked Dr. Medoff the same question. He said there's no known cure now, but they're trying to find one."

Struggling over the words, I forced myself to ask the question the answer to which I dreaded most to hear. "Did he say . . . how long . . . Ricky . . . might . . . live?"

Dad was nodding, but unable to speak right away. His drawn face revealed how chagrined he was to be the bearer of such painful news. Finally, he said softly, "A few weeks, a few months at the most, he couldn't say for sure."

I knew it was breaking Dad's heart to have to tell me that.

"Does Margie know?"

"Not yet. Dr. Medoff said he just didn't have the heart to break the news to either one of you. That's why he called me and asked me to tell you. It's obvious that he thinks the world of you and Margie, and he was practically crying when he told me."

"Poor Harold . . . He and his wife have become good friends, and we see a lot of each other socially. He is a wonderful doctor, and he really cares. The children love him. He has been coming to see Ricky regularly. I can understand his not being able to tell us. I'm sure it was hard enough for him to have to tell you."

"Yes, but now you have to break the news to Margie."

"I know, and I dread it. And you'll have to tell Muv. I hope it won't upset her too much . . . But now I've got to go back to Philadelphia right away."

"I'll drive you to the station, whenever you're ready."

"Okay, Dad."

As I walked slowly back to my office, I felt as if my priority system had come crashing down on me. All of the things that just a few moments ago had mattered so much—the press releases, the speaking engagements, the stat sheets, the promotions, the publications, the fan mail, the special events, all the busywork that demanded my attention and ruled my daily life—suddenly seemed much less important. My priorities had been rudely and instantaneously reordered by the heartrending news that my son was dying. How instantly precious to me became the gift of life that I had always taken for granted.

Johnny Myers was still there when I returned. I had been gone only a few minutes, but it felt like an eternity. I must have appeared to be in a daze, because Johnny immediately asked me, "What's wrong, Dick?"

"Ricky has leukemia. Margie doesn't know it yet. I've got to go back to Philadelphia." I found myself fighting to hold back the tears.

With that, Johnny said, "Come on. I'll take you."

I tried to demur, but my friend insisted. "You need company," he said. "Besides, you'd do the same for me. Let's go pick up whatever you need."

It was more a command than an offer, and so, with my father's grateful concurrence, I left with Johnny. We had a wonderful conversation all the way to Havertown, during which I did most of the talking. Johnny proved himself to be a sensitive listener, as I spoke about Ricky and wrestled aloud with the implications of his terminal illness. The trip was therapeutic for me.

It was about 5:30 p.m. when we arrived at the Emacks' front sidewalk. Sensing my need to be alone with Margie, Johnny politely refused to come into the house, saying that he really should get back to Baltimore. After waving goodbye to my friend, I walked up to the front door and rang the bell. It was Margie who opened the door. She was totally surprised to see me, and knew instantly that something was amiss. One look at my face told the whole story. Without saying a word we just stood there in the doorway and hugged, comforting one another. After a few moments I told her about Harold's call to Dad, and then she told me that Harold had mentioned the possibility of leukemia earlier that day, so my confirmation was not as much of a shock as it might have been, though it was just as painful.

Ed and Ruth Emack were, as always, the most gracious hosts and insisted on delaying dinner in order that we might go immediately to the hospital to see Ricky. We took Ellen with us and had a brief but beautiful visit with Ricky, who had already captured the hearts of everyone in the children's ward.

After dinner Margie and I drove to the Medoffs' house, where Harold gave us the whole sad story. We spent the entire next day at the hospital with Ricky, with time out for lunch with Harold, who introduced us to the specialists who were involved in Ricky's case. One of them commented, "If it were known that someone would get leukemia next week or next year, there would be absolutely nothing anyone could do to prevent it. At this point in time, we don't know what causes it, and we don't know how to cure it. I'm sorry, Mr. and Mrs. Armstrong, but that's just the way it is."

While we were at the hospital Dr. and Mrs. Childs telephoned Margie from Brazil, having received her telegram about Ricky. They were sorely distressed not to be with us in our time of need. Dr. Childs was on a year's leave of absence from Princeton University, while teaching at the University of Rio de Janeiro. Margie's younger sister, Martha, was with them.

That was Friday, June 4, 1954. The next day Margie and I drove to Baltimore for the weekend to take up where the movers had left off at our new house on Lochwood Road. Andy and Ellen remained with the Emacks, and Margaret Niles, the widow of the former pastor of Margie's home church, who was now living in Bryn Mawr, Pennsylvania, spent the day with Ricky at the hospital. A longtime friend of the Childs family, Mrs. Niles was now serving as parish visitor for the Bryn Mawr Presbyterian Church, where Margie and I had occasionally worshiped and attended social functions. Margie had telephoned to tell her about Ricky, and in her sweet, caring manner Mrs. Niles insisted on devoting her day to Ricky when she learned of our having to go to Baltimore.

With the help of our faithful friend Johnny Myers, who worked with us much of the weekend, we managed to ready the house for occupancy. Pleased with our progress but weary from our intensive labors, we climbed into our car Sunday evening for our long drive back to Havertown. I returned to Baltimore by train the next morning. Two days later Harold Medoff told Margie, who immediately telephoned me, that Ricky could leave the hospital the next day. Margie met me once again at Thirtieth Street station, which is very close to the University Hospital. We stayed with Ricky until visiting hours were over, and then returned to the Emacks' for a late supper and another long night of conversation.

The next day we attended Ellen's graduation from nursery school in the morning, brought Ricky back to the Emacks' that afternoon, packed the car, waved goodbye to these friends who had been so kind to us, and headed for Baltimore. That night the five of us were together for the first time in our new home.

June 9, 1954, Havertown. We had just attended Ellen's graduation from nursery school and now were dropping her off at the Emacks', who had been babysitting Andy. Margie and I would then drive down to the University of Pennsylvania Hospital to get Ricky, who was to be discharged that day.

June 9, 1954, outside the University of Pennsylvania Hospital. Ricky was so happy to see us!

Ellen and Ricky were glad to be together again. They were always very close and got along beautifully.

10

Ricky

Now, sixteen months later, I had respectfully bowed out of my last official function with the Orioles in order to stay home and help Margie care for Ricky, whose condition had greatly deteriorated in the last few days. Thanks to cortisone and one other "miracle" drug that had become available, Ricky had been able to lead a relatively normal life until quite recently. He had had several good remissions. Whenever the drugs would cease to be effective, he would quickly begin to go downhill. Then would follow agonizing pain, and a new dosage would be prescribed in an effort to halt the leukemic process.

Occasionally Ricky would have to go to the hospital for blood transfusions. In the later months the heavy doses of cortisone had caused his body to become so bloated that it was always a struggle for the doctors to locate a vein in which to insert the needle. Several times they were forced to probe around in his arm for twenty minutes or more before the transfusion could begin. Not once did Ricky cry, even when we assured him it was not any less brave to do so. To have us tell him he was a brave boy made him exceedingly happy. He wanted to make us proud, and we could not have been more so.

We knew that Ricky was embarrassed about his appearance, although he never showed his discomposure. It hurt us terribly to hear him teased by adults who should have known better. We were walking out of a restaurant one day, when a woman who had been sitting at the next table said in a deliberately loud voice to her young son as we walked by, "See what happens when you eat too much? You don't want to look like that, do you?"

Ricky outwardly appeared to accept such comments good-naturedly. But one incident sufficed to make us realize that beneath his cheerful exterior his little heart was often breaking. On this particular occasion I could tell something was bothering him. Ricky had been playing with some other children. At first he declined to answer my questions. With great reluctance he finally confided to me that one of the children had said "a very bad word. He said I was . . . fat." The way Ricky spoke the word, I knew it was a terribly painful word to him.

Yet Ricky got along well with children of all ages. The barrier that his altered appearance caused in making new friends would always be quickly dispelled by his kindness and cheerful disposition. Shortly after we moved to Princeton, I was working in another room of our apartment, when I heard the living room door open and shut. Then all was quiet. Hearing nothing after that but Ricky's heavy breathing, I went to see what the matter was. At my persistence, Ricky finally told me what had been going on. Apparently he was being put through his usual initiation by some of the seminary children. When I offered to intercede, Ricky's response was, "No, Daddy, I think it would be better if I would take out some of my toys and let those boys play with them. Then we can all be friends."

Ricky had become a great baseball fan in Baltimore. He was a good little athlete himself and was remarkably well-coordinated for a five-year-old, until his disease slowed him down. His favorite player was Willy Miranda, the Orioles' popular shortstop. One night I took Ricky with me up to the broadcast booth. While he was there a foul ball was hit back into the booth by none other than Willy Miranda. Ricky sighed longingly, "I wish I could get a ball like that."

What a happy little fellow he was when the man who had recovered the ball brought it over and presented it to Ricky—the very ball his hero had hit! One of the press photographers came over to Ricky and said, "I wonder if you would let me have that ball for my little boy. Your father works for the Orioles, and he can get you another ball."

Ricky looked to see if the man was in earnest. "But Willy hit this ball," he said, as if there could be any other ball in the world quite like that one.

"I know he did," replied the photographer, "but won't you let me take this one home to my little boy? He doesn't have a baseball."

It was a real test. I alone knew how much that ball meant to Ricky. Another one would not be the same. He looked at me as if to apologize for what he was about to do, and then handed the ball to the man. "Okay, you may have it."

I could have hugged him right then and there. Instead I whispered in his ear, "Good boy, Rick!" The man put the ball in his pocket and started away. Then he turned around and handed it back to Ricky. "Here you are, son, I'll get another ball from one of the players. You keep this one."

Ricky saved photographs of the players. He knew each player by name and number, and he treasured their pictures and cards. The last time he was in the Princeton hospital for a transfusion, he overheard a woman reading the sports page to her twelve-year-old son, who was in a bed across the ward from Ricky. "I bet he would like to have some of my photographs!" Ricky exclaimed, and he insisted that I bring in his folder, so that he could pick out some pictures to offer to his fellow patient.

It was that same day that two of the children in the ward were crying continuously, mainly from homesickness. Ricky diagnosed the trouble. It bothered him to hear them cry, and he expressed his feelings to Margie: "Mommy, why doesn't someone explain to those boys about being in the hospital?"

Ricky loved to have us there and hated to see us leave when the visiting hours were over. But he never cried or complained. He understood. He wanted all children to have that understanding so that they would not be so unhappy about being in the hospital.

I used to hate it whenever I had to tell him that he must go into the hospital again. For Ricky it meant more pain and suffering and being apart from us. I would take him aside and talk with him "man to man." He always listened to reason. "Sometimes we have to do things we don't like to do, Ricky," I had said to him on one of his early visits to the hospital. "God gives us a chance to show how brave we can be, and that's how we learn to be better people. You're getting your chance when you go to the hospital."

The most recent time I was more apprehensive about telling him than I had ever been. We both remembered his last experience at the Union Memorial Hospital in Baltimore, when some incompetent intern had completely botched the blood transfusion. I don't know what would have happened had not Margie and I been standing there during the procedure and called attention to the alarming swelling in Ricky's arm. Being present was a precautionary step we had learned to take when something similar happened months before.

This time, when I said, "Ricky, let's go into the other room a minute; I need to talk with you about something," he looked at me and smiled. "You don't have to tell me, Daddy. I know what you're going to say. You want me to go back to the hospital again. I don't mind." It was as if he were trying to comfort me instead of the other way around.

While he was taking cortisone, Ricky was on a very rigid diet. Salt was strictly forbidden. Cortisone always stimulates one's appetite, and when he had the desire to eat, he was not allowed to have the things he really would have enjoyed. At supper one night he was eyeing the potato chips longingly. "Mommy, do you think I could have just three of those?"

"You may have them Ricky, but you mustn't ask for any more, because they have salt in them, and you know you're not supposed to eat food with salt."

Ricky hesitated. "I guess I won't have any then, Mommy," he said finally, adding with a sigh, "but I do love potato chips so much."

We shall never know what Ricky thought about it all. The frequent trips to the doctors, the special diet, the pills, the shots, the transfusions, the pain—all of that could not fail to make a powerful impression on a child his age. Our constant theme with Ricky was that sooner or later everyone suffers some kind of illness. "Some people have trouble with their eyes," I tried to explain to him during one of our talks. "Some have ear trouble. Others have heart trouble. Your trouble is blood. Sometimes you get the wrong kind of blood cells and you have to be treated, just like a person who has some other kind of trouble. Another thing, Ricky, many children don't get a chance to learn how to be brave, and then when they get older, it's much harder for them. You're having your troubles early."

During one of Ricky's painful periods, I bought him several miniature cars. Late at night I would put one of the cars by his bed, so that he would see it first thing in the morning. For a couple of days he was in such pain that he could scarcely lift a finger. At one point Margie decided to get out one of the cars, which he had not yet seen. He was too weak even to hold it, but he smiled. "Now will you put it back, Mommy, so Daddy can give it to me in the morning?" He did not want to deprive me of the pleasure of our little game.

When we asked Ricky how he felt, he would usually reply, "Fine." Only in the last few days had he begun to say, "Not so well." He felt our concern, but he never took advantage of it. As soon as he would start to feel better, Ricky immediately wanted to do things for himself. He refused to be treated as an invalid. If I was away, even when it was sheer torture for him to move, he would crawl up the stairs to bed, rather than allow Margie to carry him. "I'm too heavy, Mommy," he would say.

We could hardly stand seeing him struggle up the stairs, one step at a time. I finally realized that he thought he was being a burden when I carried him. "Ricky, I wish you would let me carry you. Some day you'll be such a big boy that I won't be able to carry you any more. It would make me happy if you would let me carry you now." That did it. Ricky did not want to deny me that pleasure. From then on I carried him. We worked out a method that was the least painful for him.

We wanted very much for Ricky to have the experience of going to school. Ever since his sister Ellen had started he had looked forward to the day when he would be old enough to go. Ellen entered the first grade in Princeton, and normally Ricky would have been starting kindergarten. Both Margie and I felt, however, that there was nothing in kindergarten to stimulate Ricky's incredibly creative mind. He already colored and drew beautifully, built intricate structures with his blocks, was adept at putting together model ships, cars, and planes, and was extremely clever at cutting out little paper figures, which he himself would design. He had started to read, knew many of the multiplication tables, and could add, subtract, and tell time. From the age of three he had been able to pick out pieces on the piano by ear. Later he taught himself to play with both hands, playing the melody with his right hand and three-part, harmonic chords with his left.

Ricky's memory was unbelievable. He knew from where and from whom every toy he ever owned had come, and where every piece belonged. Whenever anything was misplaced in the house, we could count on Ricky to find it for us.

We were convinced, therefore, that Ricky was intellectually ready for school. We faced a problem, however, inasmuch as Ricky was not old enough to be admitted into the first grade and had never had any formal schooling. We made an appointment to see Mr. Chester Stroup, principal of the Princeton Elementary School, and presented the situation to him.

"We don't usually admit children who are under our age limit," Mr. Stroup informed us, "but in view of the circumstances we might be able to work something out. Will you make an appointment to have Mr. Jack

Bardon, our school psychologist, test Ricky, so we can see if he would be able to do first grade work?"

On the morning of September 14 Mr. Bardon came to our apartment to administer a series of tests to Ricky. The next day, even that very afternoon, would have been too late, for Ricky took a serious turn for the worse that day. As it was, he did not feel well at all in the morning, and by the middle of the afternoon he was in great pain and hemorrhaging badly. Still, the interview with Mr. Bardon was the highlight of his young life. He loved every minute of it, even though he was not able to do as well as he could have done, had he been feeling better. Mr. Bardon had invited Margie and me to sit in on the interview, and each of us was feeling upset, as we heard Ricky miss questions we knew he could have answered under normal circumstances. We were desperately wanting him to do well enough to be able to go to school.

A few days later we met with Mr. Stroup and Mr. Bardon at the school to discuss Ricky. Mr. Stroup informed us that he had made arrangements for Ricky to be admitted on whatever basis was convenient for us and suitable for Ricky's health. "We don't normally discuss the testing results with parents," he went on to say, "but in your case I have asked Mr. Bardon here to share his findings with you."

Mr. Bardon then proceeded to describe in detail the findings from his two-hour session with Ricky. I wish I could put into words our feelings, as we listened to this Jewish psychologist talk about our son. All I can say is that it was as if God were speaking directly to us through the lips of a man we hardly knew. Becoming more and more animated with every word, he told us things about Ricky we had always known to be true, but which we never thought anyone else could understand or appreciate. Because this stranger, a professional, could discern the same qualities that we saw in our little boy, it was as if God were justifying our parental pride in Ricky's giftedness and confirming our valuation of his unique qualities. We heard God saying to us through Mr. Bardon, "You are right to feel the way you do about Ricky, because that's the kind of child he is."

Margie and I were individually experiencing exactly the same feelings as we listened to Mr. Bardon. That is the nature of the radical spiritual and emotional rapport that has always existed between the two of us. We knew, without saying a word, that God had given us a precious gift that morning, and that what was happening in Mr. Stroup's office was more than that for which we had hoped, the acceptance of our child's readiness for school. It was for us a faith-confirming testimony to the grace, love, and mercy of God, a God who knows and who cares.

Later Mr. Bardon sent us a copy of the written report of his interview with Ricky. It read in part as follows:

> It is almost impossible to describe the productivity and amazing perceptive skills this child showed. He had the ability to see a scene or an object or a test item and immediately sense all the various aspects of what he saw. He could be critically literal in his productions and yet add some special touch, from his own imagination, which captured the special flavor of what he saw. Along with this, his motor skills were highly developed, as was his ability to deal with spatial relations.
>
> As we went along, I myself began to get excited, as I saw him perform on items way beyond his expected potential. From two tests which give I. Q. approximations, Ricky had mental age scores of 9 years and 10 months and 9 years and 3 months, giving him an I. Q. score in the 170s. The significant aspect of this, however, was the quality of his responses. He was responding like a bright nine-year-old. This great intellect and maturity of approach in his little body, with his little voice and obvious 5-year-old mannerisms was for me a stimulating experience.

In our subsequent conversations with Mr. Bardon we were impressed that he was able to discern and respond to what we called Ricky's spiritual sensitivity, which I am thoroughly convinced is a gift of God. It is the capacity for being kind, considerate, polite, understanding, responsive, caring, and Christ-like. The person who has the gift of spiritual sensitivity is one who has deep insight into the motivations of other people and reacts to them in the most beneficial way, who relates to people in a manner that brings out the best in the other person, who has genuine sympathy and compassionate love for others, and who recognizes, identifies with, and responds to the things that pertain to God. Spiritual sensitivity is that indescribable, compelling quality wherein something of the divine nature is revealed in a person.

It was Ricky who first made me aware of this quality, which was so beautifully reflected in his life. He had a depth of understanding and sensitivity to the moods and feelings of other people that revealed an astonishing maturity of character. Although his talents were many, what impressed us the most was his responsiveness to our moods, our desires, and even to what we thought were our disguised feelings. He seemed to sense what we were thinking before we expressed it, and his ability to anticipate our wishes was uncanny.

Ricky willingly accepted or assumed responsibility. When he was three and a half he announced one day that while I was working in Baltimore, he would be the man of the house and take care of things. This was not just a child's idle promise, soon to be forgotten. Ricky lived the role, week after week. Since the cleaning function had been largely mine, keeping the house tidy became one of his main projects. Day after day he would get up early, make his bed, then straighten the entire downstairs before Margie got up. Whenever they went to the store, Ricky would insist on walking on the outside, declaring, "that's what men do."

His concern about our lifting him, therefore, was totally consistent with his sensitive consideration for others. That was all the more reason why Margie and I wanted so much for him to have the experience of going to school. The willingness of the school to accept him was thrilling news to Ricky. Unfortunately, he was now too sick to take advantage of it. As I carried him up to bed after supper, I wondered if he would bounce back enough to fulfill his wish, if only for a few weeks or a few days.

That night Margie was able to go to bed early and sleep, while I stayed up with Ricky, who was in deep physical distress. I tried my best to make him comfortable, holding him as gently as I could and softly talking him through the recurrent surges of pain. The morphine that he had been taking probably alleviated but did not eliminate his misery. About three o'clock in the morning he began vomiting and passing blood. Several times I had to carry him into the bathroom. In the midst of one torturous effort on the toilet, Ricky put his arm around me and said, "I love you so much, Daddy."

About 3:30 a.m. I carried him into our bedroom and laid him on our double bed. He was breathing with difficulty, but still conscious and able to respond. Margie, who had been sleeping fitfully in the other bedroom, awoke and came in to be with us. She immediately sensed the seriousness of Ricky's condition. While she stayed with Ricky, I went down the narrow staircase to our tiny living room and telephoned Dr. Munro. "Ricky is very, very sick," I said, after apologizing for arousing her at that hour. "Could you possibly come? He may be dying."

Dr. Munro explained, very regretfully, that her ailing mother was with her and could not be left alone, and suggested that I call her associate, Dr. Benjamin Silverman. We had met the young Princeton pediatrician on one of our office visits with Dr. Munro. "He knows about Ricky, and you can tell him how to get to your apartment."

Dr. Silverman did not seem the least bit disturbed by my wake-up call and said he would come immediately. "Thank you so much, Dr. Silverman. It's 100 Stockton Street, the large cream-colored building perpendicular to the street, entry J, apartment 1. I'll leave the door unlocked so that you can come right in. We'll be up in our bedroom with Ricky."

I hurried back upstairs to find Ricky barely conscious. In a few minutes he lapsed into a semicoma. I was holding one of his hands and Margie was holding the other. We kept saying, "Mommy and Daddy are right here with you, Ricky. We love you. We're here. And God is here. We love you, Ricky. We're with you. We love you."

I gently slid my arm beneath his head as his breathing became slower and weaker. At 4:00 a.m. on September 27, 1955, Ricky's valiant struggle ended.

A moment later we heard the door open downstairs. It was Dr. Silverman. We called to him to come up. One look at our faces was all the greeting he needed. With a nod and a smile, he immediately bent over the bed to examine Ricky. He then stood, and looked at us, shaking his head. "He's gone. I'm sorry."

Dr. Silverman called the Mather Funeral Home for us, and by six o'clock they had come and taken away Ricky's body. When we called to tell Margie's parents, who had returned from South America on July 16, and who had been keeping our other two children for the past few days, Margie's mother inquired, "What time did you say it was when Ricky died?"

"Four o'clock."

"That's just when Ellen woke us up. I went into her room, and she was sitting up in bed and calling out Ricky's name! She kept saying over and over, 'Ricky! Ricky! Ricky!' It took me several minutes to comfort her and get her back to sleep."

Margie and I were grief stricken, as one would expect. Even though we knew that sooner or later this day would have to come, Ricky's death was a shock to us, nevertheless, for we had no way of knowing it would happen when it did. I kept saying to Margie, "What if I had gone to Baltimore last night? I would never have forgiven myself. And to think how close I came to going!"

But God did not let me go. For me that will always remain another gift of God's amazing grace. Let the unbelievers thank their lucky stars for such a miracle. I choose to give the credit and the praise to the God who alone can make such things happen. Let the cynics scoff at those who think such incidents are anything other than coincidence. I choose to see them as the confirming evidence of the goodness and mercy of God. It was not chance that kept me from going to Baltimore that night, when I had every intention of going, and there was every reason to go. I knew then and I know now that it was God and God alone who stopped me in my tracks. There is no other explanation that can satisfy the undeniable logic of my faith in a God who in everything is working for good with those who love God.

I was so tired from lack of sleep and so numb with sorrow that I felt more like a zombie than a live human being when I wandered over to Miller Chapel that evening to attend the opening convocation of Princeton Theological Seminary's 144th year. Margie was too tired to attend, but had insisted that I go, believing it would help to ease my sorrow. I have a vivid recollection of that service. I can even picture where I was sitting in that packed chapel, and I recall my feelings as Dr. Mackay in his welcoming remarks extended the sympathy of the seminary community to "one of our new students and his wife, whose little boy died this morning." At first I felt as if the words I was hearing were about someone else, someone I did not know. Then came the awful realization that it was Ricky, Margie, and I about whom Dr. Mackay was speaking!

Years later I tried to recapture those feelings in a poem titled, "Convocation Day." Poetry and music have always been for me means of expressing thoughts that plain words somehow could not convey, and so I include it here as a way of describing what was going on inside me that unforgettable night:

CONVOCATION DAY[1]
Are these my thoughts, or are they dreams?
The voice is real,
and yet I feel
beyond the reach of any well-intended word
I may have heard
but did not really hear.
So near
the vocal sound, and yet so far
from my half-conscious mind, it seems.

---

1. This poem first appeared in my second volume of poetry, titled *Now, That's a Miracle!* (CSS, 1996). It is written in iambic tetrameter but formatted to reveal the irregular rhyming scheme.

A Sense of Being Called

My mental door is left ajar,
as in a stupor, vaguely sensing all
yet feeling not at all.
My dry, unblinking eyes are seeing naught,
as though they have been caught
in some weird state of flux between
reality
and fantasy,
while I am bound
with chains unseen
by those around,
who, far from mean,
are quite transfixed by words addressed
to them but nonetheless expressed
in unfeigned sympathy
for me
because our son has died
this very morn—their convocation day.
Why am I sitting here this way?
Because, resolved
to be involved,
I forced myself at last to come.
My body, mind and soul are numb.
I have not cried
as yet.
I feel as if I'm in a kind of trance,
aware enough to dare
to hope
by some divinely ordained chance
that this indeed is one nightmare
from which I shall awake
to find our son still there.
But my heartache
is much too strong,
though all along
his Mom and I have known this day
would come.
Still we had hoped by some
much prayed-for miracle of grace
that God would spare our son,
whose face
is in my mind's eye clearly now.
The speaker's voice announces how
"One of our students and his wife today

Ricky

have suffered a great loss,"
and something else about a cross.
Then, for some reason, suddenly
I'm jolted from my reverie
by my harsh rediscovery
that all these words of sympathy
are meant for Margie and for me.
It is *our* son whose death is news
to all the strangers in these pews.
The voice confirms my saddest fears,
and now I'm fighting back the tears.
The muscles of my throat are sore
from swallowing the lump. What's more,
I feel a claustrophobic urge
to rush out from this crowded place.
I'm on the verge
of screaming, No!
It can't be so.
I can't erase
the awful truth, and yet . . .
and yet
there's still a shade
of disbelief that will not fade,
nor will it let
me rest at ease until I know.
Is it false hope, or morbid fear,
or grief compelling me to go?
The friendly greetings that I hear,
as I push through the parting crowd,
are answered with a weak, forced smile,
but not aloud. And all the while
my heart pounds with anticipation,
not in hopeful expectation.
It's as if some heartless fiend
has gleaned
a devilish delight
in tempting me
to think tonight
that Ricky might be there,
and thus propelling me
by hope
that soon would turn into a deep despair,
a cruel trick, the kind
a sadist plays upon a tortured mind.

A Sense of Being Called

The tempo of my heartbeat
now is faster than my running feet,
crossing the lawn, as I have done
so many times to see my son.
Then bounding up the concrete stair
and pushing wide the door, I stare
into the darkness of the room,
where normally there is a light.
But not tonight,
for Margie is exhausted by her long ordeal.
She did not feel
that she could go with me
to such a convocation.
Having had to bear the brunt of Ricky's recent tribulation,
she has gone for days
and days
with very little sleep or rest,
and both of us had thought it best
that she stay home instead.
Since she is now in bed,
I gently close the door,
and then, I do the same
as I have done so many times before:
I softly call his name.
It's not that I
think he'll reply,
but that I must now play again
the little game
we played, we two,
which in the final days I knew
would have to come to this,
a sad pretending, like a lover's kiss
bestowed upon the breeze,
to sadden, not to please
the heart,
which, though about to break,
must from the start
indulge its pain
for love's sake.
So I wait in vain,
suspended in the silent void,
to hear once more the bravely cheerful voice of one
I so enjoyed
and loved, reply

"Hi, Daddy!" to be followed by
my "hello hug." But now
I feel the agonizing absence. Yet somehow
I cannot let myself believe our little boy is gone.
My loving wife will comfort me
and I her, and we both will see,
that life goes on,
as people say,
and convocations like today,
while she and I,
so painfully bereft
are left
to wonder,
Why?

Our *why* was not the why of anguished despair or of self-pity, directed to a God whose concern we doubted and whose absence we resented. It was a question not about God's presence but about God's purpose, the teleological *why* of faith. What did God want us to learn from and to do about this experience of grief? Our question was the natural corollary of our constant prayer that somehow we could see even in Ricky's suffering and death that God was working for good. In the trauma of bereavement, the question became suddenly paramount.

It was a question that would be answered in God's time.

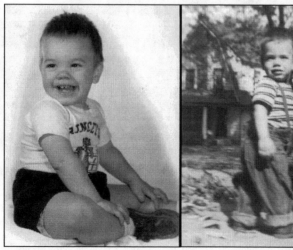

Ricky at twelve months was a merry little fellow.

Ricky at eighteen months on the front walkway at 2440 Linden Drive.

June 23, 1953. Ellen and Ricky are enjoying their backyard "swimming pool"!

Ellen (3½) and Ricky (2½) are modeling the new coats they got at the Coatcraft Factory in Philadelphia.

Above: Ellen (4½) and Ricky (3½) are having a "Tea Party;" Ellen is saying grace.
Left: Andy and Ellen had blue eyes. Ricky had brown eyes like his mother's.

Andy joined the team on January 13, 1953. Here he is at eight months.

Above: Ricky and Ellen with neighborhood friends. Playing in the snow was always fun.
Left: Ricky (3½) is a wonderful big brother to nine-month-old Andy.

July 16, 1954. We are standing on the lawn of our home on Lochwood Road. Ricky was still in his first remission but was beginning to show the physical effects of his cortisone treatments. We were about to leave for the Dulles International Airport to meet Margie's parents and her sister Martha, who were returning that afternoon from Dr. Childs' year-long sabbatical in Brazil.

July 16, 1954, Dulles International Airport. Welcome weary travelers! How excited the children were to see their Grampy and Granmama again! There were many rounds of hugs.

November 1954. This was our last family photo with Ricky.

Above: August 11, 1954, Mago Vista Beach, Maryland. My Aunt Nora, affectionately known as "Ooah," took Martha, who was visiting us, and the children to this spot on the Magothy River. Because of the sea nettles, the children spent most of the time playing in the sand, which suited Ricky (4⅓ years old and still in remission) just fine. Ooah was glad to have Martha along to help her. *Right*: December 25, 1954. Ricky hadn't been feeling too well.

A Sense of Being Called

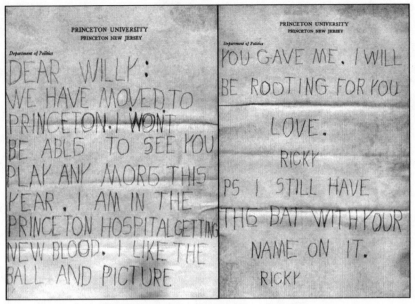

DEAR WILLY:
WE HAVE MOVED TO
PRINCETON. I WON'T
BE ABLE TO SEE YOU
PLAY ANY MORE THIS
YEAR. I AM IN THE
PRINCETON HOSPITAL GETTING
NEW BLOOD. I LIKE THE
BALL AND PICTURE YOU GAVE ME. I WILL
BE ROOTING FOR YOU
LOVE.
RICKY
PS I STILL HAVE
THE BAT WITH YOUR
NAME ON IT.
RICKY

September 2, 1955. Ricky composed and printed this letter just before he went into Princeton Hospital. I took it with me to Baltimore and hand delivered it to Willy, who very thoughtfully returned it to us after Ricky died twenty-five days later.

Willie Miranda, the Orioles' popular short-stop, was Ricky's favorite player.

New York Yankees

EXECUTIVE OFFICES · 745 FIFTH AVENUE
NEW YORK 22, N. Y. · PLAZA 9-5300

BUSINESS AND TICKET OFFICES · YANKEE STADIUM
BRONX 51, N. Y. · CYPRESS 3-4300

September 16, 1955

Ricky Armstrong
100 Stockton Street
Apt. J 1, South Hall
Princeton, New Jersey

Dear Ricky:

Your Dad tells me that your two favorite Yankees are Mickey Mantle and Yogi Berra. They were both happy to hear that they are among your favorite ball players, and they have asked me to send you these two pictures with their special good wishes on them to you.

Hope you are feeling fine and that your whole family is enjoying Princeton.

Send them my best regards.

Very truly yours,

Robert O. Fishel

ROF:r

Near the end of the 1955 season I had a conversation with my Jewish friend and counterpart with the New York Yankees, Bob Fishel, who not long afterward sent this letter to Ricky, enclosing autographed photos of two of Ricky's baseball heroes, Mickey Mantle and Yogi Berra.

A Sense of Being Called

Some of Ricky's Drawings

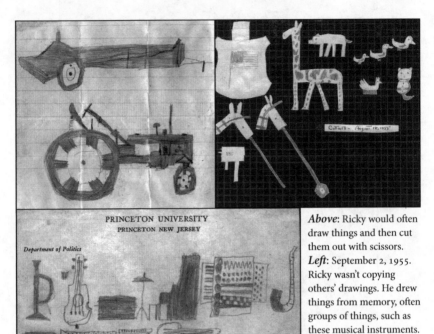

Above: Ricky would often draw things and then cut them out with scissors. **Left**: September 2, 1955. Ricky wasn't copying others' drawings. He drew things from memory, often groups of things, such as these musical instruments.

Above: May, 1955. Ricky's attention to detail was amazing. **Right**: Unfortunately these black and white reproductions do not show Ricky's remarkable use of color. He drew this picture with crayons on September 3, 1955, three and a half weeks before he died.

11

Two Visits to Maryland

The funeral service was held the following Friday morning in the Niles Memorial Chapel of the First Presbyterian Church. The chapel was named for the former pastor who, along with Margie's grandfather and my cousin Maurice, had married Margie and me. Maurice drove up from Havertown that morning to conduct the service, which was a beautiful testimony to God's providence and love and to Ricky's brave spirit. In retrospect our one regret about the service was that the casket was open. No one had advised us to the contrary, and so we had to stare throughout the service at the body of our little boy, while we tried to concentrate on what was being said. Even so, as we sat holding hands in the front pew, Margie and I felt the peace that passes understanding, though our hearts were heavy with grief.

We were grateful for the support of those who came to the service. Margie's parents and some of their friends were there, along with a few members of the seminary community. My father had driven up from Baltimore the day before to be with us, but my mother was not well enough to make the trip. Margie and I had learned how therapeutic it is to talk about a loved one who has died, as we sat with her parents and my dad in the parlor of the Mather Funeral Home the night before and reminisced about Ricky's life. It was the best preparation we could have had for what was to follow the next day, when we would watch our son's little casket being lowered into the ground.

119

Niles Memorial Chapel holds many memories for me. This is where the memorial service for Ricky was held, and where I would later teach the junior high Sunday school class for a year.

After the service we stationed ourselves at the rear of Niles Chapel to greet and thank those who had come, while the undertaker was taking the casket out to the hearse that would transport Ricky's body to Baltimore for burial in the Armstrong family plot in the Lorraine Park Cemetery. Shortly after that our two-car caravan pulled out of the church parking lot behind the hearse for the three-hour drive to the cemetery.

There was just a hint of the glorious fall foliage that before too many more days would bedeck the wooded slopes of Lorraine Park Cemetery. As we approached the tree-covered hill where my father's parents were buried, we could see the tall figure of Ren Jackson standing near the open grave. Ren had very kindly agreed to conduct the committal service, for which a number of my Baltimore relatives and friends had already gathered. The gentle September breeze that whispered through the oak trees was like a soothing balm to our aching hearts, and Ren's caring, thoughtful words blended with the peaceful setting to renew our spirits and restore our perspective. Ren had known Ricky and understood as well as anyone our feelings for our son. The committal service was a fitting closure to Ricky's short life and a benediction to us.

My aunt Nora Stoll, who had been like a second mother to my brother and me all our lives, had a delicious dinner for Margie, me, and other members of the family in her apartment that evening. After that we drove back to Princeton. We talked about Ricky all the way home. That too was therapeutic.

Ten days later I was back in Baltimore again for a quite-different occasion. This time it was to meet with the Committee on Candidates of the Baltimore Presbytery. I had applied to be taken under care of the Presbytery at the time Margie and I joined Faith Presbyterian Church. Having received the endorsement of the session and in consideration of my situation the committee kindly telescoped the constitutional process so that I could appear at their morning meeting on October 10 and be recommended to the Presbytery that afternoon. I had completed all the application forms, obtained the necessary letters of recommendation, and taken the series of psychological tests required of all Presbyterian candidates.

The forty-five minutes with the committee was a spiritually enriching experience for me. What I had feared might be a rather intimidating examination was a time of faith-sharing and warm Christian fellowship. The members listened sympathetically and compassionately to my responses to their questions, and their comments were supportive and encouraging. One of the persons there was the Rev. Dr. A. Brown Caldwell, whom I had known before. As stated clerk of the Presbytery he had written me a very cordial letter in June, recalling an earlier meeting: "When I sat with you at the Optimist Club in the Lord Baltimore Hotel some months ago, and talked with you about sports and especially the Orioles, it could not have entered my mind that you would be seeking this calling as you are now doing. We are eager, in the Presbytery, to do all in our power to aid and further you and your family."

Lorraine Park Cemetery, near Baltimore, Maryland

I was invited to leave the room while the committee discussed my candidacy. After a few minutes they called me back and informed me that they would recommend that I be taken under care of the Presbytery as a candidate for ordination. Following a beautiful prayer by one of the committee members, I was excused. I had a warm feeling in my heart as I closed the door behind me, having had my first taste of what it means to be under the care of a committee that *really* cares.

A Sense of Being Called

That afternoon Ren Jackson drove me to Frederick, Maryland, for the meeting of the Baltimore Presbytery. Once again I was asked to share my faith story, this time with the entire Presbytery. When I think back upon that experience, I am amazed that no one asked me any questions, for in my statement I made no reference to Jesus Christ. If the Presbytery had judged me on the basis of my Christology, I would never have been approved, and perhaps I would not be in the ministry today. I could not speak about a personal relationship with Christ, nor was his name part of my vocabulary. That relationship was yet to be discovered and developed. Fortunately for me, the subject never came up, and so I was unanimously received as a candidate under the care of the Presbytery of Baltimore.

Driving back to Baltimore that evening, Ren and I had so much to talk about that it seemed to take no time at all to reach the railroad station. Ren parked the car so that we could continue our conversation on the platform, while waiting for my train to arrive from Washington. What a good friend he had become! And what a tremendous support he had been to Margie and me in our journey of faith. So much had happened since that late-night visit in early May. We talked about Ricky, of course, and I was glad to have the opportunity to tell Ren again how much we appreciated his committal service.

For his part, Ren wanted to know how things were going for us at seminary, especially since Ricky's death. He asked if my grief made it hard to concentrate on my studies, and whether it had affected my sense of purpose about being there. I assured him that my sense of call was as strong as ever, and that I was studying as hard as I could. But we did miss Ricky terribly and always would. You never get over the death of your child, but, as they say, "You learn to live with it."

On the train to Princeton I welcomed the opportunity to reflect on the events of the day and on all the changes that had taken place in my life. Could I ever have imagined a year before that I would now be in seminary, studying for the ministry, under the care of the Presbytery of Baltimore?

And could I have guessed that my mother and father would now be church members? Their decision to join Second Presbyterian Church in the Roland Park section of Baltimore was wonderful news to me and a beautiful testimony to the fact that the Holy Spirit had used my call to touch the lives of my parents. My mother and father had always been believers, and they lived their faith. But from the day they were married they had never joined a church. "I figured it was about time we did," my dad had laughingly said to me, "with a son going into the ministry. We talked with Dr. Warren about it, and he was most helpful. We really like him, and we like the church. He understands that Muv is not able to attend, but I've been going pretty regularly."

The Rev. Dr. Paul C. Warren, as chairman of the committee on candidates, had been very helpful to me when I was applying to be taken under care of the Baltimore Presbytery. I am sure my parents knew how happy I was about their decision to join the church, and especially the church of which Dr. Warren was pastor. It added another dimension to the relationship between my parents and me, for now we could talk to each other as fellow Presbyterians!

These were some of my thoughts as I listened to the click of the train wheels whizzing along the tracks.

12

A Whole New World

Although the pain of our loss was difficult to bear at times, Margie and I knew we could not go on grieving. During the day there were too many things to be done and busy schedules to meet. But at night I would lie in bed thinking about Ricky. There was also the delicate task of interpreting Ricky's death to our other two children, Ellen and Andy. In their own way, they missed him as much as we did, and they were just as eager to reminisce about him.

Not having attended most of the opening week of classes, I had some catching up to do that weekend, and I was grateful for the help I received from my classmate Sam Calian, who had taken copious notes, and his brilliant roommate, Dale Bruner. Remembering them as students, I was not surprised when years later Sam became president of Pittsburgh Theological Seminary and Dale a distinguished biblical scholar and professor at Whitworth College. They were among the many excellent students at Princeton Seminary. Indeed, I was immediately impressed by the high academic caliber of my classmates, the majority of whom in those days came to seminary directly from college. Unlike the situation in most seminaries today, there were only a handful of second-career persons, of whom I was one of the oldest, and there were comparatively few married students. That too has changed, as the ratio of married to single students has nearly reversed.

With as skimpy a background in religion and theology as I had, I found myself in my notetaking at the beginning of the term having to spell many of the lecturers' words phonetically. Most of the time I was able to find the words later in my theological dictionary, but sometimes my spelling was not close enough to locate a word. Then I would have to swallow my pride and ask someone. In his required course in Ecumenics, Dr. Mackay was continually using a word that I simply could not find, so at the conclusion of his lecture one morning I went up to the podium. "Excuse me, Dr. Mackay, but my theological vocabulary is rather limited. I need help in identifying a word I've heard you use a number of times in your lectures, but I can't find it in my dictionary. My phonetic spelling hasn't worked in this case. It sounds like 'perfit.'"

Dr. Mackay's expression was somewhere between amazement and amusement. "Perfet? Perfet? You can't spell perfet?"

"No, sir. I can't find it in my dictionary. How do you spell it?"

The look on Dr. Mackay's face was now a combination of disbelief and annoyance. "Perfet: p-e-r-f-e-c-t—perfet!"

My red face must have betrayed my embarrassment, as I mumbled my apology and slunk away. "Oh! I guess I misheard you. Thank you, Dr. Mackay." I was never sure whether Dr. Mackay realized I was serious, or whether he thought I was calling attention to his Scottish accent; for Scots, I learned, say "perfet"!

Despite my linguistic deficiencies in the early days, adjusting to the rigors of the seminary curriculum was not as difficult as I had feared it would be. Attending classes was, in fact, an exhilarating experience for me, as I found myself studying subjects unlike any I had ever had in my undergraduate days. A whole new world was opening up, and I could not bear the thought of missing a single lecture or preceptorial. I can remember thinking and commenting to others that what we were studying would be invaluable even if we were not preparing for ordination. Just to begin to think theologically and to study history from a Christian perspective had a transformational impact on my entire worldview. For the first time in my life the Bible was coming alive for me. I had professor Howard Tillman Kuist primarily to thank for that. His yearlong course in the English Bible helped me to get a grasp on the content and structure of the Scriptures, and his enthusiasm for the Word of God was contagious and thrilling.

What made all of the courses so interesting and meaningful was the commitment of the professors to their subjects and their genuine concern for their students. Our instructors were persons of faith, who believed in the God they talked about, and whose conviction as servants of Christ matched their competence as scholars. They were my role models as well as my mentors, and they instilled in me a zeal to learn and the recognition that my theological education must continue for the rest of my life. How it bothered me to hear some students express their boredom with this or that course or professor. They were not smart enough to know how much they did not know.

One thing that soon became powerfully clear to me was that I had to come to grips with the person of Jesus Christ. Near the beginning of that first term one of the more evangelical students asked me when I had found Christ. I remembered feeling uncomfortable with the question and even a bit resentful at the time. "I didn't know he was lost," I replied, quoting a retort I had heard from someone else. That ended the conversation, and I felt bad about it later. The poor fellow had meant no harm. He was just try-ing to engage me in a faith-sharing conversation, and I should never have responded so cynically.

The truth was that I had not found Christ, and I knew I could never be a Christian minister until I had. I knew I had been called to be a minister, but it was not a Christ-centered call. At least I did not think of it as such. Who was this man called Jesus? And how could I preach and pray in Jesus's name if I did not believe him to be the divine Son of God? How could I proclaim him Lord of the universe and Savior of the world if I did not know him as my personal Lord and Savior? Was he or was he not the Christ? I could not ignore the question. I realized I had to decide, or quit seminary. It was as serious as that.

I wanted to believe. With all my heart I wanted to believe, but I was not sure I could. For me it was an intellectual as well as a spiritual chal-lenge. I just could not make myself believe that this Jewish carpenter's son could somehow be the Savior of the world. Throughout that first term I kept praying to the God I did believe in, the God who had called me into the ministry, for the faith to believe in Jesus.

I cannot pinpoint the time and place when it happened, but I know that my prayers were eventually answered. Sometime between then and the time I graduated from seminary I came to believe that Jesus Christ is in-deed the Savior of the world and my Savior, the Lord of all life and the Lord of my life. It has happened to me exactly as he said it would: "The Advocate, the Holy Spirit, whom the Father will send in my name, will teach you everything, and remind you of all that I have said to you . . . He will glorify me, because he will take what is mine and declare it to you" (John 14:26; 16:14 NRSV).

In other words, the Holy Spirit has testified in my heart that Jesus is who he said he was, and who the church through the ages has proclaimed him to be. I know that is an affirmation of faith, and that my faith in him is a gift of God. As he himself said, "No one can come to me unless drawn by the Father who sent me" (John 6:44a). The Apostle Paul echoed that truth when he wrote, "No one can say 'Jesus is Lord' except by the Holy Spirit" (1 Cor 12:3b).

I came to Christ through an intellectual door. No one evangelized me. It was the logical outcome of my theological education. I am sure that my new awareness of and appreciation for the authority of the Bible had much to do with my coming to Christ. I remember the first time the Bible really spoke to me. I was reading the book of Acts late one night when it suddenly dawned on me that I was reading holy history. The idea that the Holy Spirit could speak to a believer through the words of Scripture was no longer just a theoretical possibility. It was happening to me that night. I was so excited that I immediately got down on my knees and thanked God. From that moment on, the Bible has been my source of inspiration, the authority for every word I've ever preached, the rule for my faith and practice. It is the Word of God to me.

I did not realize at the time how much my own faith struggle would affect my future approach to evangelism and my style as a witness to and communicator of the gospel. Now I know how my theology has been shaped by my Christology. I believed in God before I ever could talk about a personal relationship with Jesus Christ, but now I can say that it is through Christ that I have come to know what God has done and can do for us, and what God expects of us. I have discussed this at length in my other writings, but for now I simply want to put my faith struggle into its proper context. I have also tried to express it in the following little poem:

Looking Back[1]
My call to be a minister
I never will forget.
In retrospect I know my faith
was not Christ-centered yet.
I spoke not of a "call of Christ"

1. "Christology Delayed" first appeared in my book, *The Pastor-Evangelist in the Parish* (Westminster John Knox Press, 1990).

nor thought about it much;
I should have been quite mystified,
were it described as such.
A personal relationship
with Christ I couldn't claim,
and it was even hard for me
to pray in Jesus' name.
It truly was a call of God;
there's no doubt in my mind,
but putting it in terms of Christ—
those words I could not find.
I came to know the living Lord
on seminary sod,
and now my faith in Jesus Christ
informs my faith in God.
From God to Christ, from Christ to God,
thus with the Spirit's aid
by providential grace was my
Christology delayed.

Despite my faith struggles, Margie and the children were settling into the life in Princeton. Ellen was thriving in the Nassau Street Elementary School, while Andy was home with Margie. There were no daycares in those days, but there were plenty of willing babysitters available. Thus Margie found time to become involved in the seminary women's activities and in the Princeton Wellesley Club. She also started a part-time job, working three nights a week as a file clerk in a local medical office in order to supplement our income. Our across-the-hall neighbors, the Baileys, or one of our other friends, or Margie's parents, would babysit for us whenever I was not available. It was wonderful for us and the children to have their Grampy and Granmama so close, and we saw them often. Margie talked with her parents by telephone or in person almost every day. On Sundays we attended First Presbyterian Church, where the children were enrolled in church school.

Spring 1956. All dressed up for Sunday school.

Often I would work in the development office in the evening and study in the later hours. My friend Frank Watson, a

West Point graduate and former jet pilot, who was a second-year student (a middler) at the seminary, and I found a perfect hideaway in a boarded-up section of Tennent Hall, where we could study undisturbed.

During the day, when I was not in class I was in the office, where there was always plenty of work to be done, including the planning and implementation of a major fundraising campaign for the new seminary library. In addition to working on that time-consuming project, I was given the responsibility for figuring out the formulas for the seminary's deferred gift plans, supervising the annual-giving campaign, preparing the public relations and development brochures and other promotional literature, editing the *Spire* (mailed quarterly to 140,000 names), answering certain correspondence, and many other related chores, all subject to the final approval, of course, of my genial boss, Dr. Quay, who spent much of his time calling on donors.

We worked well together and had great conversations, during which I probably learned as much about ministry, theology, and the church as I did in the classroom. He was a delightful storyteller, a perceptive analyst of human nature, and a keen observer of the world scene. Members of the seminary touring choir, who regularly heard him preach when he traveled with them on their weekend visits to churches, were constantly praising Dr. Quay's sermons. I felt exceptionally privileged to be able to work with and for such a man.

I felt privileged also just to be in a community where people were concerned about the weightier matters of faith and life, and where in the midst of a healthy theological diversity one could work out one's own convictional salvation with fear and trembling. What was especially exciting to me was the continual experience of discovering the relevance of the Christian gospel for daily living. I kept thinking about the secular world out of which I had come and the religious apathy of so many of the people I had known. I remembered them well, because I had been one of them. Though I had given up alcohol out of respect for Margie's convictions, I had no qualms about writing jingles for beer and wine companies. Though I was personally opposed to gambling, I had planned the best advertising campaign I could for a major racetrack. The discrepancy between my professional practice and my professed values had never occurred to me. I cannot remember ever talking about God or religion with anyone in the advertising world. That is not to say there were no religious people in advertising. The subject simply never came up. If the people with whom I associated had any strong religious affiliation, they never mentioned it, nor did their religion have any apparent bearing on their convictions, values, language, lifestyle, or goals.

The same was true, in those days at least, of the world of professional sports. Organizations like the Fellowship of Christian Athletes and the Baseball Chapel had not yet been formed. Many athletes and sports executives were believers, of course, but the prevalent lifestyle could hardly have been called Christian. The more I studied, the more aware I became of the need to find ways to communicate the gospel to the secular world. I began to sense that my call to ministry was to do precisely that. Having lived and worked in the secular world, I felt that perhaps I could share the good news in terms that same world could hear and understand, people like my friends in the press box.

My first attempt to explore this possibility found expression in a lengthy term paper titled "Professional Sports as a Missionary Frontier," which I wrote for Dr. Mackay's course in ecumenics. The paper was read by Dr. Mackay's young teaching assistant, David Crawford, who, it just so happened, was a rabid sports fan. He told me later that in the midst of all the esoteric theological titles among the many papers submitted, my topic had immediately caught his eye. His enthusiastic response to my thesis was just the encouragement I needed as I thought about my calling in relation to my theological studies.

Dave Crawford and I quickly became good friends. There were others, including members of the faculty and their spouses, like Virgil and Phyllis Rogers, with whom Margie and I often played bridge for relaxation; and many of my fellow students. Margie and I enjoyed getting together with our dormitory neighbors and others, and our life at Princeton Seminary was most pleasant.

Two of my married classmates with whom I often studied for exams were Mac Freeman, a brilliant Canadian who was attending seminary on a scholarship from the Rockefeller Theological Foundation, and Bart Leach, an all-Ivy League basketball star from the University of Pennsylvania who had turned down a potentially successful career in pro basketball in order to study for the ministry. We used an empty lecture room in the Christian education section of North-South Hall, where there happened to be a piano. Invariably we would take a break for some terrific late-night jam sessions, with Mac blowing a mean trumpet, Bart using an inverted metal wastebasket for a drum, and me tickling the ivories. Early on we feared we were disturbing our neighbors in the apartments, when they began pounding on the walls. When I went to apologize, they said, "Oh, please don't stop! We were trying to get your attention to see if we could request some songs for you to play."

There were other opportunities for me to indulge my love of music, including singing in the seminary's nontouring choir. In return for that commitment, the choir members were awarded the privilege of private voice lessons from the incomparable James McKeever. Our choir sang in the chapel service every Wednesday.

Not long after we moved to Princeton I was contacted by Wat Stewart and Dick Sly, former members of the Princeton Nassoons, with whom I had also sung in my undergraduate days at the university, about forming a local men's singing organization. We had no difficulty recruiting ex-Nassoons, ex-Whiffenpoofs, and assorted other college glee clubbers and alums of various campus singing organizations for our new group, which we promptly named the Palmer Squares, a play on the name of the central square in downtown Princeton. With that kind of talent, we developed very quickly into a fine, close-harmony singing group and soon had mastered a sufficient repertoire to begin accepting engagements. I did not begrudge the evening rehearsals or the engagements, which were a refreshing, fun-filled change of pace from my seminary work-study routine.

So was the seminary's well-organized intramural sports program, in which our dorm participated with a vengeance. We married students field-ed an impressive team in the touch-football league, but I must confess that it was more than a little intimidating the first time we stared across the line at big Donn Moomaw, the three-time all-America linebacker from UCLA. The intramural basketball league was even more impressive, for most of the players had competed in college, including several all-conference players and three all-Americans. It felt good to be involved in competitive athletics again.

My ties to the baseball world were not completely severed, as I contin-ued to receive letters and telephone calls from former colleagues and friends. Among the latter was Don McClanen, who soon became my most frequent correspondent. I agreed to draft a public relations/fundraising plan for the Fellowship of Christian Athletes. Because of my job at the seminary, I was unable to accept Don's invitation to attend the FCA's first national confer-ence in Estes Park, Colorado, in 1956; but I agreed to become a member of the national board of directors.

"FOR KICKS": That's why these nine gentlemen gather together each Monday night to sing good close harmony. They are "The Palmer Squares" and they have sung, for kicks, at Princeton cocktail parties, dances and similar intellectual gatherings. They also meet frequently with other cultural groups, exchanging songs and arrangements, and they have even inspired their wives to form a close-harmony group of their own. Left to right: John Green, Charles Townsend, Alex Buck, John Yardley, James Affleck, William Hamilton, Richard Sly (who partook in a different kind of singing last Sunday as tenor soloist in Stainer's "Crucifixion" at the First Presbyterian Church); Richard Armstrong and, at the piano, William W. ("Watt") Stewart. (Town Topics Photo by Hank Chachowski)

Topics Of The Town

—Continued from Page 12

THE PALMER SQUARES

Close, Close. Once a man has sung close harmony, he'll never be really happy out in the open. That's why nine Princeton citizens have joined together in joyful enterprise, calling themselves "The Palmer Squares."

In this happy assemblage there are six Nassoons, a Tigertone, a lone Whiffenpoof and a maverick from Lafayette College. All are now alumni, of course; junior executives who relax each Monday evening with a few bars of "How Can I Tell Her?" "Goin' Home Train," or that fine old madrigal, "Whoopie."

The Squares were first blocked out in June, 1956 by William W. ("Watt") Stewart, Jr., who modestly says that the catchy name was thought up "mutually" by the group because it sounded Princeton-ish.

At first, the Squares were an octet, but they now number nine and they are eager for more. Anybody who sings bass or tenor—especially tenor—will be interviewed with great enthusiasm. The chief requirement is a background in close harmony or barbershop singing.

The group is more or less homogenous: some of the members knew each other before; all had sung before. Besides Mr. Stewart, who was a Nassoon, they include Richard Armstrong, John Yardley, Richard Sly, William Hamilton, and James G. Affleck, all Nassoons; Charles Townsend, an ex-Tigertone; John Green, the Whiffenpoof, and Alex Buck who had sung at Lafayette.

Besides the operatic selections mentioned above, the Squares' repertoire includes a classic, "East of the Sun," and such folk melodies as "Perfidia," and "Lady Be Good." Their proudest possession is an original, written for the Squares by Richard Armstrong, Seminary student and first tenor. It's called "I've Had My Worries" and reflects little of the Seminary influence.

The Squares have no arranger, as such; they take arrangements where they can, learning some from music, some by ear. A rehearsal starts at 8:30 Monday night and lasts, technically, for three hours. Does it ever go on all night? Said a spokesman for the group, "Yer durn tootin'!"

CONTEST WINNERS

This photo of the original Palmer Squares appeared with an article in *Town Topics*, Princeton's popular weekly newspaper. We expanded our ranks as we became better known in the greater Princeton area.

In the meantime, there were, throughout that first year, many invitations from churches and other organizations to share my personal testimony. I was happy to accept such speaking engagements whenever I could, but I declined all invitations to preach. I wanted to have a year of seminary under my belt before taking on any preaching assignments. Having done a considerable amount of public speaking as a baseball executive, I was not the least bit nervous about speaking at youth rallies, men's breakfasts, and church dinners. Leading a congregation in worship was something else. I knew I would have to take the plunge sooner or later, but the prospect of doing that for the first time was frightening. Despite my anxiety, I accepted the invitation of our neighbor, Al Bailey, to substitute for him on Sunday, July 29, 1956. That assignment marked the beginning of another important phase of my theological education.

13

First Steps in Ministry

Having decided to bite the preaching bullet, I accepted several other pulpit engagements in nearby churches for the remaining weeks of the summer of 1956. I needed the experience, and there was no better way to get it. My nervousness about my debut as a worship leader was aggravated by my apprehension about having to write several sermons while trying to keep up with my work in the development office *and* the summer Hebrew course, which I had decided to take. Students had dubbed the course "Kamikaze Hebrew." Anyone who has had to cram a yearlong biblical language course into ten weeks knows why!

The long-feared Sunday when I was to substitute for the Rev. Mr. Bailey at his church in Mount Airy, New Jersey, finally arrived. My daughter, Ellen, now seven years old, wanted to come with me, and I was delighted to have her company. Margie did not come, having recently given birth to our third son. She had been sick for most of the nine months with both Ellen and Andy, and this pregnancy was no different. Because of her natural aversion to hot weather, she had been feeling more and more miserable as the summer progressed.

Margie was the first to declare, however, that the safe arrival of William Harwood Armstrong was well worth any discomfort he caused her along the way. Woody, as we had already decided to nickname him, made his appearance at the Princeton Hospital on July 9, 1956. We have some wonderful home movies of his older sister and brother, who were leaping and squealing with excitement as we drove up to the door with their new baby brother.

Their excitement had not abated in the three weeks since Woody's arrival, and I was pleasantly surprised that Ellen was willing to leave him in order to come with me on my first preaching engagement. Andy and Margie were waving goodbye to us as we headed out the driveway on the 29th. It took us about forty minutes to reach our destination. I can picture the little white country church on that hazy, hot Sunday morning. I was greeted by an elderly gentleman who handed me a bulletin and showed me where I could put on my borrowed seminary choir robe. Ellen seated herself in the center of the front pew, looking very pretty in her Sunday dress, yellow bonnet, white stockings, and patent leather shoes, and behaving like a proper little lady.

After inspecting the pulpit, introducing myself to the organist, and inquiring about the procedure for the offering, I withdrew to the little room behind the chancel and used the remaining minutes to look through the order of worship and go over my sermon one more time. As the fateful hour approached, my tension was mounting, the same tension I used to feel before the referee blew the whistle for the opening kickoff, or the umpire shouted "Play ball!"

Finally it was time to enter the sanctuary. Armed with my sermon manuscript and the church bulletin, I took my seat in the big wooden chair behind the central pulpit and waited for the prelude to end. I had written a call to worship, which I read without incident. Following the opening hymn there was an invocation, concluding with the Lord's Prayer. The invocation was also written; the Lord's Prayer was not. That was my first mistake. As an Episcopalian-turned-Presbyterian, I had been concentrating on remembering to say "debts" instead of "trespasses" and I managed to get it right, only I went on to say "as we forgive those who trespass against us." So discombobulated was I by my having succumbed to force of habit, that my mind went completely blank on the last part of the prayer, and I could not remember which came first—the glory, the power, or the kingdom. It was obviously disconcerting to the congregation for the worship leader suddenly to stop in the middle of a unison prayer. But, bless their hearts, they stumbled on to the end.

A little later in the service we said the Apostles' Creed. That was something else I thought I knew by heart, having been saying it all my life. But when we got to the last six "I believes," I became hypnotized by the sound of the congregation reciting the creed. Instead of leading, I started listening, and my mind went blank again. I could not remember what I was supposed to believe, and so I just waited it out. I sensed that the congregation was more amused than annoyed, knowing that I was "only a seminary student."

Then came the offering. After handing out the plates, I took my seat again. Almost immediately I was conscious of a pair of vigorously waving arms. I sneaked a peak around the side of the pulpit and discovered the arms belonged to my daughter, who was trying desperately to get my attention. I shook my head and gave her a look intended to make her sit still. Then I tried to get out of her sight by slumping down behind the pulpit. That did not deter Ellen, who slid to the extreme left end of the pew and angrily glared at me, as one of the ushers handed her the collection plate. I had forgotten to give her some money for the offering! The usher should have been able to size up the situation and move on to the next pew, but he just stood there. I leaned to my left to escape Ellen's view, whereupon she slid to the extreme right end of the pew, where the other usher was waiting for the plate. Then in a stage whisper that surely could be heard by the entire congregation, Ellen said: "Daddy, no money!" The ushers grinned and moved on, finally. What I should have done was go down and give her some money as soon as I realized what the problem was, and had I been more comfortable in my role, I would have done so. For the next few minutes Ellen sat with her arms folded, sullenly staring at the floor or angrily glaring at me. During the next hymn we exchanged smiles, and I knew that all was forgiven.

After the hymn I remained at the pulpit and waited for the congregation to be seated for the sermon. I had memorized the familiar words from Psalm 19 for my prayer before beginning to preach, but what came out was, "Let the mords of my wouth . . . " I knew that was wrong, so I started again. "Let the mords of my wouth . . ." Somehow I just could not get it right, so I finally said "Amen!" and started preaching. By the grace of God, the sermon seemed to go well. At least, the congregation was attentive and responsive in spite of my inauspicious beginning. Regardless of their impressions, that service was a memorable experience for me.

Ellen and I had much to share, when we returned home that afternoon, but Ellen soon became preoccupied with her baby brother. Woody's birth was the highlight of the summer for all of us, of course, and indeed of the entire year. Ellen, who has always loved babies, was a tremendous help to Margie in caring for the newest member of our family, and I did my share of diaper changing and bottle-feeding. One of my regular parental

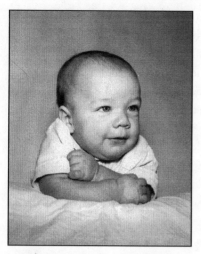

Meet the newest member of our family, William Harwood Armstrong, born July 9, 1956. Ellen (off camera) had no difficulty getting her two-month-old baby brother's attention for this snapshot. Woody has already discovered he has an adoring older sister and brother.

duties with each of our children had always been the late-night bottle-feeding, and Woody was no exception to the practice.

The addition of Woody to our family circle necessitated some changes in our family routine, but there was still Hebrew to contend with, my job to perform, and Sunday preaching engagements to be kept. Now that my preacher's feet were wet, the rest of my guest preaching assignments that summer were less traumatic but not without mishap. On one occasion in a divided chancel I went to what I thought was the lectern to read the Scripture lessons and discovered that I was in the pulpit. That would have been no problem except that there was no Bible in the pulpit! Not wanting to call attention to my dilemma, I recited the lessons from the RSA Version, a rather loose paraphrase of the RSV. I got the impression the congregation did not know the difference!

In another church on a stifling Sunday in August we were in the middle of the responsive reading when a freight train roared by only a few yards from the open windows of the church. It seemed to take forever, as the cars kept rolling by. I could not hear the congregation, and the congregation could certainly not hear me. We kept on, nevertheless, trying to read each other's lips and body language to tell when to start each response. When the noise of the train finally subsided, I figured we must be near the end of the selection, so I read my final part as loud as I could. The congregation came in on cue with their responsive reading, and the organist then played a brief introduction to the *Gloria Patri*, which everybody sang as if nothing at all irregular had happened. That led me to conclude that the freight train was no stranger to them. I just wish somebody had warned me about it in advance!

Near the end of the summer my family and I were able to spend two weeks in a tiny cottage in Surf City, New Jersey, in return for my preaching on two successive Sundays in the little community church there. I had my speech professor, Dr. Bill Beeners, to thank for the invitation and Dr. Quay to thank for allowing me to have the two weeks off from work. He realized that was the only vacation we had had since we left Baltimore.

We had fun building sandcastles, riding the waves, and strolling along the beach. Our friends Ruth and Ed Emack drove over from Philadelphia to spend two long weekends with us. We somehow managed to find sleeping space for our two families, but our two-month-old son Woody saw to it that none of us got too much sleep. We had lots of fun, nevertheless.

The Surf City and other preaching engagements that summer were a refreshing change of pace from the demands of my regular job and the pressure of keeping up with the Hebrew course. The weeks sped by, and suddenly it was autumn. Having successfully completed both the Greek and the Hebrew language requirements, I was relieved, relaxed, and ready for my middler year to begin.

Not far into the fall term I had another unforgettable experience that had nothing to do with my studies or preaching. It was October 8, 1956, when the New York Yankees and the then-Brooklyn Dodgers were scheduled to play the fifth game of the World Series. Observing my nervous fidgeting,

Dr. Quay very kindly shooed me out of the office early that afternoon so that I could watch the last few innings of the game on television. I was especially eager to know what was happening, because a former Oriole, Don Larsen, had been named surprise starter for the Yankees. The game was in the fifth inning, when I arrived at the apartment and turned on the TV. Margie and the children were not home, so there was no one to whom I could voice my excitement when I discovered that Larsen had a no-hitter going. In fact, he had not allowed a single base runner in the first five innings!

I was so excited that I could not sit down, as Larsen mowed the Dodgers down in order in the sixth, seventh, and eighth innings. By the start of the

Don Larsen as an Oriole in 1954, when his record was 3 wins and 21 losses. Who could have imagined that two years later the lanky right-hander would pitch a perfect World Series game for the New York Yankees!

ninth inning I could hardly stand it. I was holding my breath with every pitch. The gangling ex-Oriole was on the verge of pitching the first perfect game in World Series history. What an utterly incredible feat, if he could accomplish it! Not one fan in Yankee Stadium that afternoon could have been rooting any harder for Don Larsen than I was, despite my acquired dislike for the team that had dominated the American League for too many years. As an American Leaguer, however, I rooted for whichever team was representing the Junior Circuit in the World Series—even the Yankees. And this day I had a double reason for wanting them to win.

Carl Furillo was the first batter to face Larsen in the bottom of the ninth. After fouling off several pitches the Dodger right fielder hit a routine fly ball that was easily put away by his Yankee counterpart, Hank Bauer. One down, two to go. The next Dodger batsman was the ever-dangerous Roy Campanella, who for the first four games of the series had been hitting the ball well. Larsen, who had been pitching without a windup all afternoon, sneaked a fastball in for a strike, but on the next pitch Campy connected with one. I gasped as I watched it sail high and deep toward the left-field stands. But with my next breath I let out a loud shout of relief, as the ball landed in foul territory among the upper-deck fans. Strike two! That close call only heightened my anxiety. But on the very next pitch, Campanella grounded weakly to Billy Martin at second base. Two down, one to go!

Larsen had now faced and retired twenty-six men in a row. He was one out away from pitching a perfect game. Could he do it? Not if Dale Mitchell had his way! Mitchell was sent in to pinch hit for Dodger pitcher Sal Maglie, who had hurled an excellent game in his own right, well enough to win most ball games. Larsen's first pitch to Mitchell was a ball.

"Oh no, Don! Don't walk him!" I yelled, as if the Yankee pitcher could hear me through the television set.

Larsen fired another fastball to Yogi Berra. Mitchell was taking all the way. "Strike one!" barked home-plate umpire Babe Pinelli.

"Yeah! That's the way, Don!" I screamed. One and one. Larsen hummed another fast one, and this time the Dodger batter took a ferocious cut at the ball—and missed! Strike two.

"Whew!" I gasped. "One more, Don! One more! Just one more!"

Mitchell stepped out of the batter's box to regroup. I had been standing in front of the TV from the moment I turned it on. Now I hardly dared to breathe. My fists were clenched and raised like a boxer's. "Come on, Don! Come on, Don! Come on, Don!" I whispered through my clenched teeth.

Mitchell was back in the box. Larsen got the signal from Berra. Then, still without a windup, the big Yankee right-hander let go with another blazing bullet. The ball cut the corner of the plate and smacked into Yogi Berra's big mitt. Up went the umpire's right hand. "Strike three!" Don Larsen had accomplished the impossible—a perfect game in the World Series!

Yankee Stadium erupted. If the fans were not pounding and hugging one another, they were applauding wildly and shouting their approval. The Yankee players went berserk. Yogi rushed out to the mound and leaped upon the jubilant pitcher. I wanted to stay and watch the celebration, but I could not contain my excitement. I had to share the experience with someone else—anyone. I rushed out of the apartment and down the entry steps expecting to find the other residents as eager as I to discuss the incredible feat we had just witnessed. But there was no one in sight. Where was everybody? Did they not realize what a phenomenal event had just occurred?

Disappointed and puzzled, I was about to go back inside, when a woman, whom I recognized as the wife of one of the doctoral students, emerged from another entry, carrying a laundry basket. I ran up to her excitedly. "Did you see it? Wasn't that incredible?"

"See what?"

"The World Series! Don Larsen just pitched a perfect game! It has never been done before and probably will never happen again! Think of it: twenty-seven men in a row, not a single base runner! I never thought I'd live to see it. A perfect game! Imagine that, a perfect game!"

The woman looked at me disdainfully. "I couldn't care less," she said in a tone of sheer disgust, and went her way.

Talk about having your balloon punctured! If that exchange had taken place a year earlier, I might have quit seminary right then and there. Not really, for it had not taken me long to discover that being a seminary student did not preclude one's right to get excited about baseball. I was too stunned by the woman's squelch to say anything. Not until she had walked away did I think of several mean retorts, and that was fortunate for both of us. The old "press-box needler" in me was ready to rear his ugly head. I thanked God for not letting that happen, and upon further reflection, I was also grateful to God for the object lesson that sour-faced woman had provided in how *not* to relate to anyone who wants to share something about which he or she is excited. She had unwittingly provided further confirmation of my conviction that Christ's ambassadors need to relate to people where they are, just as Jesus himself did. Pastors cannot afford to be uninterested in the things their people are excited about. That's the best way to be both boring and irrelevant, not to mention insulting.

Further contact with that same woman revealed that she was a rather unhappy person with a singularly unpleasant personality. Like the woman in the familiar ballad, she was more to be pitied than censured, and I dreaded to think what life would be like for her and her husband in a parish.

Despite that unpleasant occurrence, I was feeling in a very positive mood about things in general. The much-maligned middler year seemed manageable at first, but it soon proved to be no less pressure-packed than my junior year had been. Now I had weekend fieldwork to contend with, along with everything else! The good news was that I had accepted a position as student assistant minister at the First Presbyterian Church of Princeton, with responsibilities for the junior high program. I had started working there on a volunteer basis in the spring of 1956 with Bob Howland, a seminary senior, who was hoping the church would ask me to take over after he graduated. They did, and I was delighted to accept. Never had I dreamed that I would be working in the church of the pastor who had advised me to remain in baseball! Both John Bodo and I remembered the conversation well. Many months later he referred to it in a letter I received from him: "I still remember how I tried mildly and non-directively to talk you out of becoming a minister. I believe that in retrospect you will understand why I said then what I said. I wanted you to be 100 percent sure that this was the only thing you *could* do. Now you have proved it—at least to me—beyond a doubt."

Working with the youth fellowship at First Presbyterian Church was Margie's and my first opportunity to be in ministry together. I taught the junior high Sunday school class, and the two of us worked with the officers and advisers to plan and carry out an ambitious program for the junior high fellowship. Our introduction to youth ministry was a totally positive experience. We learned much, made some lasting friendships, and thoroughly enjoyed working together as a couple.

My contact with John Bodo that year was limited. He was a hands-off supervisor, who rarely appeared at any of our fellowship activities. I'm sure he read my reports and knew what was going on, but he left me entirely to my own devices, and I liked it that way. If I had a request or needed his permission to do something, he was always accessible. Otherwise I saw him only in worship on Sunday mornings. We had one or two staff get-togethers, but they were strictly social.

Because of my fieldwork responsibilities I was unable to do any guest preaching throughout that year, but there were many opportunities to speak on other than Sunday mornings. And there was the ordeal of preaching my middler sermon before a class of my peers, to be critiqued by a professor of homiletics and one of the speech instructors. When I had finished my sermon, having exceeded the allowed time limit, I sat down in the front pew and awaited the message of doom from professor Donald Macleod, who by the time he retired had listened to more Presbyterian students preach than has anyone else in the world before or since. Dr. Macleod strode to the front of the chapel and stood there staring at me without saying a word for what seemed an eternity. He was searching for the right words.

"I have just one question for you, Mr. Armstrong," he said finally, with a quizzical smile on his face. "What is there left for you to preach about next week?"

Professor Macleod's other constructive criticisms and complimentary comments have long since been forgotten, but not his question. It taught me a lesson every preacher needs to remember: Don't try to say it all in one sermon!

The Rev. Dr. Donald Macleod, Francis L. Patton Professor of Preaching and Worship at Princeton Theological Seminary, had one question for me when I finished my middler sermon.

14

It Helps to Have a Sense of Humor

I had many opportunities to apply that lesson the following summer, once I had concluded my fieldwork at First Presbyterian Church. Because of my full summer preaching schedule, Professor Christy Wilson, director of field education, allowed me to count my other volunteer work at First Presbyterian Church and my supply preaching toward the field education requirement. Ordinarily a student was required to have two years of field work in two different churches or approved ministries. As much as Margie and I had enjoyed our work with the youth at First Church, we were relieved that I would not have to serve another church during my senior year. Dr. Wilson agreed that I had probably learned as much about leading worship and preaching from being a guest preacher in so many different churches as I would from being a student assistant in one church. I had not preached or participated in the worship leadership the entire year at First Presbyterian Church!

My sense of relief about being excused from another fieldwork assignment in my senior year was heightened by a totally unexpected development at the end of my middler year. I was nominated for president of the student body and, much to my surprise, was elected. Having served on the Student Council for two years, I knew how much work the presidency involved; but with Margie's support, Dr. Quay's permission, and Dr. Mackay's encouragement, I accepted.

Little did I realize how much work that responsibility would entail. In those days the Student Council had much greater authority than it has had in recent years, being responsible for planning and implementing the entire program of the student association.

One of my first "official" acts as student body president was not official at all. It took place near the end of June and involved David Crawford, Dr. Mackay's teaching assistant, who had become a good friend and with whom I had shared many laughs. Knowing that Bishop Lesslie Newbigin was scheduled to be one of the plenary speakers during the second week of the Institute of Theology, an annual event attended by three or four hundred pastors, I persuaded Dave to let me dress him up in a disguise and introduce him to the Institute as Bishop Newbigin. Using a disguise kit that Margie's sister Betty Ann had given me for Christmas in the first year of our marriage, I fitted my willing accomplice with a false nose, ears, a beard, glasses with built-in eyeballs that stared in different directions, and a wig. Clothed in a black robe and a scholar's cap, he certainly had to be the weirdest looking figure ever to appear on the Princeton campus, although there have been some that might have rivaled him for the title.

He was so weird that people were embarrassed to stare at him directly, when I would introduce him as Bishop Newbigin. Instead they would cast furtive glances his way as we moved on to our next victim. People assumed that I was assigned to be the bishop's guide in my capacity as student body president, and I said nothing to disabuse them of the idea. Our first stop was the registration desk for the Institute, where the Rev. Donovan Norquist was directing traffic. The "bishop" stationed himself just out of range of Don's clear vision, and was busy blowing the tassel on his cap, while I sauntered up to the table and asked where the bishop would be staying. "Oh, my gosh!" exclaimed the dismayed director of the Institute. "The bishop is not due here 'til *next* week. We don't have a room for him! What am I going to do?"

The Rev. David L. Crawford, after serving as a pastor for several years, returned to Princeton Seminary as administrative assistant to the president, in which role he was in my view Princeton Seminary's most effective recruiter and articulate ambassador of goodwill.

"I'll take care of it," said I, mirroring Don's concern. I then hustled the bishop out of the Campus Center and on to other venues, where the wild-haired, dark-robed figure evoked various degrees of astonishment. So far the bishop had not uttered a word. Eventually we decided to push our luck and call on one of the seminary's senior administrators, whom I shall refer to as Dr. H.

"Bishop Newbigin wanted to meet some of the seminary administrators," I explained, after we had been graciously seated by the flattered executive. He and the bishop proceeded to have a ten-minute conversation about the state of affairs in India and other weighty matters as I sat and listened attentively. Dave Crawford assumed a half-British, half-Indian accent, which must have seemed authentic to our unsuspecting victim, who, when we stood up to leave, thanked the bishop profusely for honoring him with a visit. As we went out the door, I felt a tug at my coat tail. Dr. H. was pulling me back into his office. "I appreciate your bringing the bishop down to see me, Dick" he whispered, "but I must say, he is one queer-looking duck!"

The amazing thing about that whole episode is that no one ever asked me later, "Who was that strange man posing as Bishop Newbigin, and why were you leading him around?" Maybe it was because I was on vacation the week the real Bishop Newbigin showed up! David and I kept our secret between us; but we had many a laugh about our experience. And to think that was long before Allen Funt had dreamed up his *Candid Camera* television show!

These kinds of amusing incidents enlivened the otherwise-uneventful seminary routine. I learned early on the importance, indeed the indispensability, of a sense of humor to survival in the ministry. There were sad times too, as when we would have to bid farewell to good friends, not knowing when or even whether our paths would cross again. We hated to say goodbye to Evelyn and Al Bailey, our first-year across-the-hall neighbors, and to Phil and Dora Quanbeck, who had moved into the Baileys' apartment and with whom we had become especially close. There were wonderful friends in the classes ahead of us, like Carrie and Frank Watson, Mary and Bob Howland, and many others whom we had come to know and love.

Another sad parting occurred in June when the man with whom I had worked so closely and who had been such a good friend and mentor, Dr. Quay, retired as vice president of the seminary. He was succeeded by the Rev. Joseph MacCarroll, who was appointed director of development. Dr. MacCarroll was a man of many talents, who had long years of service as a pastor and had been actively involved in the work of the General Assembly under the dynamic leadership of the then-stated clerk, Dr. Eugene Carson Blake. Although he had no previous experience as a development officer, Joe MacCarroll brought with him an encyclopedic knowledge of the Presbyterian Church, its polity, and its people. Like Jim Quay, he was an excellent storyteller, with a delightful sense of humor. The similarity between the two men, however, ended there.

We became instant friends, nevertheless, and we complemented each other's areas of expertise. I had much to learn from Joe about the politics of the Presbyterian Church and its judicatories, and Joe was grateful to have someone who knew the development ropes. My work in the office was made somewhat easier by the hiring of another student, Bill Hervey, to assist me part-time with the Alumni Roll Call, the seminary's annual giving campaign. Bill was another North Hall neighbor. We had become good friends, and when the position was approved, I recommended him as the one to fill it.

The summer went fast for our family. Early in June we had opened the Quays' cabin on a little lake near Greensboro, Vermont, and had spent two physically strenuous but mentally and emotionally relaxing weeks there. Opening the cabin entailed much more work than we expected. But there was plenty of time for swimming, hiking, boating, golfing, and reading. We spent a couple of delightful evenings with nearby summer residents and friends of the Quays, Dr. and Mrs. Eugene Carder. Dr. Carder had been the associate pastor at Riverside Church in New York City for many years. It was fascinating to hear his inside comments about Harry Emerson Fosdick and the other renowned Riverside preachers whose ministries he spanned. He spoke with passion about the role of an associate and urged me not to rule out that possibility for myself. It was not always easy, he said, to play the role of John the Baptist for a popular pulpit personality whom you did not see from one Sunday to the next.

Our activities for the rest of the summer were much the same as the previous summer. Ellen and Andy were enrolled in a nearby day camp, which they loved. I worked in the office on weekdays and preached somewhere most every Sunday. Margie still had her night job and was kept busy taking care of Woody and being a homemaker during the day. We had many visitors that summer, as we had had ever since we arrived in Princeton. Ann and Johnny Myers, Ruth and Ed Emack, Cynthia and Wilson Ballard, Don McClanen, Ren Jackson, and many other friends and relatives from Baltimore and elsewhere had spent varying amounts of time with us.

As I faced my third and last year of seminary, I had to start thinking about passing ordination exams and candidating for a church. These new concerns, along with my work in the development office, my duties as student-body president, occasional speaking engagements, singing rehearsals and engagements with the Palmer Squares, and family responsibilities promised to make the task of keeping up with my classwork in my senior year the most difficult challenge ever. Except for the grace of God and Margie's help with typing I never could have made it!

There were times along the way when we wondered how in the world we were going to make it financially. We had not been able to sell our house in Baltimore before moving to Princeton, and it remained on the market for fourteen months. Throughout that seemingly interminable period we were struggling to keep up the mortgage payments until we finally had to unload our home at a sizeable loss. Time and again we would find ourselves wondering how we were going to pay our bills, when we would receive a surprise check in the mail—a dividend from my GI insurance policy, a tax refund, a gift from a church, an unexpected honorarium, or something else out of the blue that would get us off the hook at least momentarily. Every time it happened was for Margie and me another confirmation of the amazing providence of God and of our call.

One time we were sitting at the lunch table staring at a major car-repair bill and wondering how we would ever pay it. We could not think of any possible source of funds. I remember laughing and saying, "This is one even God can't pay!" That afternoon I received a letter from my aunt Lily Bauernschmidt, my mother's sister in California, whom I had not seen since my Navy days, saying that she had been thinking about us and wanting to do something to help. She went on to say that she had received a small bequest, and being a tither, she wanted to give one-tenth to some Christian cause. After praying about it, she thought of us. It just so happened that she was a Presbyterian and since I was studying to be a Presbyterian minister, she said she had a feeling we could use the money. She wanted to share her blessings with us. Enclosed with her letter was a check for one thousand dollars!

Coincidence? Luck? Not to us! I wrote to Aunt "Billy" and told her exactly what her gift and the timeliness of it had meant to us. It was in our eyes a gift of God, not just a material gift but a spiritual blessing as well.

Despite the recurrence of such Godsends, we were forced to live very frugally. Like other student families in the same financial boat, we ate simple meals and shopped for bargains. Spaghetti was a staple; ground round was a treat. We had fewer creature comforts than we had enjoyed before, but we were never happier.

Nor were we ever more excited, as we began to see the light at the end of the seminary tunnel. The more I thought and prayed about it, the more I felt drawn to a solo pastorate, rather than to a multiple staff church. My personal desire was to be in a church where I could preach regularly. At the same time I wanted to be open to the leading of the Holy Spirit and be ready to go wherever God called me. It was not at all easy to discern God's will, but I trusted that the God who had called me and guided me thus far would eventually make it clear.

One senior pastor who had approached me about an administrative position on his staff was more than a little annoyed at me when I tried to explain, as politely as I could, that I did not feel called to such a ministry. "But you are just the person to lead our congregation in the area of steward-ship," he insisted, referring to my background in fundraising. As the pastor of one of the more prominent churches in the denomination and an influ-ential member of the seminary's board of trustees, he was not accustomed to being denied. I assured him that I was praying hard for God's guidance but that so far I was leaning strongly toward a solo pastorate. His parting comment to me was, "I'm dismayed that so many young ministers today don't know what they want to do." I let it go at that.

My wrestling match with the Holy Spirit was complicated by a persis-tent plea from Don McClanen to come to work for the rapidly expanding ministry of the Fellowship of Christian Athletes. A letter from Don dated December 17, 1957, read in part as follows:

> As you know, we have already done considerable talking about the possibility of your joining the FCA staff full time. In the days ahead we will, of course, need to further discuss and pray about this. I did, on the other hand, want to write and share with you what our Board of Directors agreed on this past Sunday . . .
>
> Realizing that it will be approximately July 1 and the start of our new fiscal year before you could possibly be with us anyway, we want you to know as of now, so that you will have plenty of time for consideration, that we extend and sincerely hope you will accept full-time employment with us as of July 1, 1958 . . .
>
> I don't know what else I can say, Dick, except that we desper-ately need what we are convinced you have to offer this program . . . I trust you will be aware of the fact that many of us will be praying

for you and with you in the important ministry of your life which
lies ahead, whether it be with the FCA or elsewhere.

It was a tempting offer, which would have enabled me to combine my
new theological training with my lifelong love of sports. Don was much
more understanding than that pastor, when I told him that as much as I
would enjoy such an exciting work, I felt called to the parish ministry. As
I wrote a few days later in response to a letter from C. L. "Biggie" Munn,
who was then athletic director at Michigan State University and chair of
the FCA's national board of directors, "When I left professional baseball to
enter Princeton Seminary, it was with the intention of entering the pastoral
ministry. Certainly it is my hope that I may accept a call where there is a
real need and where I am best qualified to serve. Whether or not it turns
out to be the FCA, I shall continue to take an active interest in this most
worthwhile program." I assured both Don and Biggie that I would give the
decision my prayerful consideration. I wanted to keep a completely open
mind to the possibility that God might be calling me to a different ministry
than I had anticipated when I entered seminary. But in my heart I still felt
called to be a pastor.

To that end I had to begin thinking about candidating for a church.
Throughout the fall I had not done any guest preaching, as the weekends
were desperately needed for studying. I could not have kept up without the
invaluable help of my wonderful wife, who typed many of my term papers.
I accepted no preaching engagements for the next two terms either, since I
wanted to keep my weekends free for candidating. There was one notable
exception, however. On January 12, 1958, I preached at Faith Presbyterian
Church in Baltimore. Ren Jackson had continued there as pastor, following
the death of his uncle, Walter T. Jackson, in February 1956. In July of that
year, however, Ren resigned in order to complete his doctoral program in
England. He had invited me to preach several times throughout my junior
year, but I had repeatedly declined. I did not feel ready to preach that first
year in my own hometown. I think Ren understood.

The Rev. Calvin J. K. Jackson, who succeeded his cousin Ren as pastor
at Faith Church, was not aware of my apprehension. He pressed me to set
a date when I could come and preach at Faith Church. Throughout my
middler year I had a legitimate excuse because of my fieldwork responsibilities. Now that I was in my final year at seminary, I knew I could no
longer postpone the inevitable. After all, I was under care of the session.
How could I refuse? I had learned very early that first summer, moreover,

that I enjoyed being in the pulpit. Planning, preparing, and preaching a sermon was the most satisfyingly creative experience of my life. So I agreed to come to Baltimore on Seminary Sunday, January 12, 1958.

The children, Margie and I drove down to Lutherville, Maryland, just north of Baltimore, the day before to spend the night with our friends Wilson and Cynthia Ballard. The next day dawned clear and cold. I left early to be at the church a half hour before the first service. Calvin Jackson greeted me warmly and led me into the sanctuary, where we talked through the service together. "The last time I worshiped here," I commented to Cal, pointing to the balcony, "I was sitting up there!"

We then went into Cal's study, where we robed. My host asked about the number in the collar of my gown, and I had to confess that I had been borrowing that same robe from the seminary choir room since the first time I preached. After a brief prayer with the church choir, we made our way to the narthex, fell in line behind the choir, and waited for the processional hymn to begin. My heart was pounding with both anxiety and excitement, as we sang our way down the long center aisle. The hour had come!

As I looked out on the congregation from my seat in the chancel, I saw many familiar faces. It was good to see them there. Still, their presence did not ease my tension, which was greater than ever, as I was sure it would be. Once I started to preach, however, it immediately subsided, and I was totally caught up in the task at hand. I do not know how good a sermon it was, but the people were very gracious afterward. Greeting them in the narthex following the service felt like old home week. There was time afterwards in Cal's study to relax and reflect on the experience. The indelible memories of that morning would not be associated with the first service, however, for the two persons who made it memorable had not yet arrived.

A brilliant engineer and one of my closest friends during and beyond our McDonogh days, Wilson Ballard was always a clever practical joker, and our mutual friend John was the innocent victim and I the unwitting subject of his wiles on that unforgettable Sunday at Faith Church.

Wilson Ballard brought Margie to the second service, having dropped off our children at my Aunt Nora's apartment on the way. An active Episco-palian, Wilson was in those days an uninhibited practical joker who took great delight in observing people's reactions to the false impressions he deliberately tried to create. When he found himself seated beside a member of the church who happened to be a business associate, he could not resist the temptation to indulge his favorite pastime. As I started to preach, he leaned over and whispered to his friend, "Who is *this* character? Why would they let somebody like *that* preach in a fine church like this? Do you mean to tell me he's the minister?"

The man was both indignant and apologetic. "He's not the minister. He's only a seminary student. He's a guest preacher."

"Oh," said Wilson, with a look of relief. "That explains it!"

Wilson could hardly wait to tell me about it afterwards. "You should have seen the expression on John's face when I introduced him to Margie at the end of the service!"

Mary Rose and Jack Dunn were also there for that service. So were Ernie and Lulu Harwell and many other baseball friends, some of whom ordinarily would not have darkened the door of any church. There were some longtime family friends, too, including Ethel and Mickey O'Neill, two devout Roman Catholics. "Efful," as I had called her when I was a toddler, had often babysat me when she was a teenager, and had watched me grow up. I had not spotted them in the congregation, but I heard Ethel's voice high above the din in the narthex. A diminutive Gracie Allen, she was a lovable character, extremely gregarious, and an incessant talker, with a distinctively high, shrill voice. There must have been a couple hundred people in the narthex as Ethel was about to come through the receiving line. Suddenly she stopped and let out a loud shriek. The whole place became instantly quiet.

"There he is in his priestly robe!" she announced to the crowd around her. "And to think that I saw him when he didn't have a stitch of clothes on!" I wonder how many of those people could guess she was referring to my infancy and her babysitting role!

No wonder that January Sunday at Faith Presbyterian Church was a memorable day for me. I was glad I had finally fulfilled my long-delayed obligation. So was Cal Jackson.

I had no other preaching engagements lined up. The next time I preached, it would be for a pastor nominating committee (PNC), which in those days was more commonly referred to as a pulpit committee.

15

So This Is Candidating!

The opportunity was not long in coming. Not many days after our visit to Baltimore, I received a telephone call from the chairman of the pastor nominating committee of the Memorial Presbyterian Church of Lancaster, Pennsylvania. He said my name had been recommended to them and asked if I would be interested in being considered. I indicated I would be and agreed to preach for the committee in a so-called neutral pulpit in a little church near Oxford, Pennsylvania, on February 23, and then to meet with the committee in Lancaster that afternoon.

It was clear and cold that Sunday, following a heavy winter snowstorm. Margie and I left Princeton at 7:30 a.m. and arrived shortly before 10:00 a.m. Members of the pastor nominating committee from Memorial Church identified Margie, introduced themselves, and sat with her during the service. Afterwards they left, and Margie and I stayed to have lunch with our host couple from the congregation. We allowed ourselves what we thought was plenty of time to drive the thirty miles or so to Lancaster for our 2:00 p.m. meeting, but we had not counted on the condition of the back roads we had to take. The snow was piled high on either side, reducing some stretches of the road to one-lane traffic. That would have been okay, except that the traffic we encountered consisted mostly of the horses and buggies of the Amish people coming home from their churches. Since there was no room to pass, we had to crawl along behind one after another until they would turn into their farms.

The result was that we were an hour late arriving for our meeting, which was to take place in the parlor of the First Presbyterian Church in downtown Lancaster. How not to get off to a good start with a search committee, we thought. The committee members, however, having guessed what might have happened, were waiting patiently and good naturedly for us. They stood and greeted each of us warmly and then invited us to sit in the two vacant chairs in the large circle they had arranged. This being our first time ever to meet with a pastor nominating committee, Margie and I had no idea what to expect. Having committed the whole process to God, we were not anxious about it. Rather we were more excited than nervous as we waited for someone to say something. I was about to suggest we begin with a prayer when the chair of the committee, a friendly gentleman named Dick Reese, who had first contacted me, began to speak. Margie and I were completely floored, when he simply announced: "Our committee has voted to call you as our minister, Mr. Armstrong!"

No questions? No discussion? No sharing of who we were and what we believed? That was one scenario for which Margie and I were not the least prepared, and I tried as tactfully as I could to communicate that to the committee. My heart went out to those dear people. They were not playing games; they declared themselves openly and honestly, right up front. I wanted them to know that I was honored by their invitation, but that I felt we had some things to discuss before I could make a decision. Then I would need time to think and pray about it. I also explained that I had already agreed to preach for another search committee, and that I needed to honor that commitment.

We then went on to talk at length about the church, their sense of mission, and the kind of minister they felt was needed as they thought about the future of their church. Mr. Reese and two other members of the committee then drove us to Memorial Church, which was only a few blocks away, and took us on a tour of the building and the manse next door. It was almost six o'clock by the time we left. Margie and I had much to talk about on the drive back home. Was this the way it happens? How will we know whether or not God wants us to accept this call? We wanted to be open, but somehow we did not feel this was the place God wanted us to be. Something was missing.

We continued our discussion until late that night and over the lunch table the next day. As usual Margie was a wonderful sounding board for me, asking all the right questions and helping me to sort out the things on my mind and heart. She was ready and willing to go to Lancaster if that was where God called me. The more we talked and prayed, however, the more convinced I became that I was not being called to Memorial Church. I could not give a clear reason why. We liked the people. We liked Lancaster. But something was missing.

Perhaps the feeling would come later, after more thought and prayer. Maybe I needed a basis of comparison. At that point I still had not talked with any other search committees, although I was scheduled to preach for the PNC of the Oak Lane Presbyterian Church of Philadelphia. Dick Reese had agreed that I needed to be sure in my heart before giving them a reply. He was perfectly content to wait until I had met with the Oak Lane committee. He understood that it was not a matter of my playing one church against the other, but of my trying to discern the will of God for my life.

In the meantime, the date had been set for me to preach for the Oak Lane committee. They had been given my name by the Rev. Dr. Earl Douglass, who lived across the street and around the corner from our dormitory, and with whom I had become very well acquainted through a mutual interest in exploring the fascinating phenomenon of unidentified flying objects (UFOs). Dr. Douglass, I learned, was a member of the board of directors of the Washington-based National Investigations Committee on Aerial Phenomena (NICAP). He had been impressed with a book-length paper I had written for Dr. Lefferts Loetscher's elective course on religious cults. Both Dr. Douglass and Dr. Loetscher had encouraged me to find a publisher for the paper, which was titled "Flying Saucer Fanatics: An Emerging Cult?" I did contact a publisher, who agreed to publish my book, provided I incorporated a history of the American guided missile program. That requirement was all I needed to scratch any publication ideas I might have had, for I had neither the time nor the expertise to tackle such an assignment.

A distinguished Presbyterian minister and author of the widely used *Douglass International Sunday School Lessons*, Dr. Douglass talked glow-ingly to me about the Oak Lane Presbyterian Church, about which he knew from his association with the Presbytery of Philadelphia. I also learned that my "kamikaze" Hebrew professor, Dr. Charles Fritsch, from whom I had taken more courses than I had from any other professor, had once served for eighteen months as the interim pastor of the Oak Lane Church. While there he met and later married a charming Sunday school teacher named Eleanor Anderson. When the Fritsches learned that I was being considered by the church, they invited Margie and me to dinner to tell us about the church and the community.

They spoke enthusiastically about the congregation but were not at all optimistic about the future of the church. "It would be a back breaker, Dick," warned Dr. Fritsch. "The community is predominantly Jewish now. There's a synagogue right across the street and several other large temples in the area. The church has been declining in membership for the last twenty years or more. At one time it was one of the strongest churches in the Philadelphia Presbytery, with well over a thousand members, but I doubt if there are two hundred active members now. From what I hear they need to do a lot of roll cleaning. I'm afraid you'd burn yourself out in a hurry. But the people who have remained members are great."

That conversation took place on March 7. A day or two later Charlie Fritsch's comments were seconded by another member of the faculty who was familiar with the church and its neighborhood. "That's not the place I would want to begin my ministry. It's a dying church. I think you'd be making a mistake to take on that kind of a challenge right out of seminary, Dick. You'd be doomed before you start."

All of this advice was being offered before I had even met the committee! What was surprising to me was that the more I heard about the challenges the church was facing, the more interested I became. Something was stirring inside me that had not been stirred before. Margie and I were getting more and more excited as we drew nearer to the date of our meeting with the Oak Lane PNC.

That finally took place on Sunday, March 16. It was a typical March day, partly sunny, breezy, and about 45° F. We left Princeton at 8:30 that morning and drove to the Mount Airy Presbyterian Church of Philadelphia, where it had been arranged for me to preach. Now that I was candidating, I was beginning to feel a bit embarrassed that I was still wearing a borrowed choir robe, but that was the best I could do. I hoped the Oak Lane pulpit committee, as they called themselves, would not judge me by what I was wearing!

Following the eleven o'clock service Margie and I met with the twelve-member committee in the church parlor. They were most cordial and friendly, and we were instantly drawn to them. The chair of the committee was W. Terry Vrooman, who invited me to begin with prayer. Terry, as he asked to be called, then traced briefly the history of the church, ending with a detailed description of their present situation. The officers and leading members of the congregation had met to discuss their plight. Should they dissolve the church, merge with another congregation, move to another location, or what? After much discussion and soul-searching, they finally decided to make one more strong effort to reverse their downhill slide. They devised an ambitious plan for renewal, which they appropriately titled "Operation Bootstrap," designed to reawaken their inactive members and to attract new members by publicizing their services and programs. These and other aspects of "Operation Bootstrap" were described in a loose-leaf notebook, which Terry flipped through for us as he talked.

"Unfortunately," said the articulate committee spokesperson, "just as Operation Bootstrap was about to be launched, our pastor left us. So now we need a minister to help us implement it."

Other members of the committee joined in the conversation in response to my questions, and I felt myself getting more and more excited. If these people were a measure of the rest of the congregation, here was a church that recognized its problems and was committed to doing something about them. They were not trying to impress us by painting a rosy picture of their situation. They were saying openly and honestly, "We have problems, and we need a minister who is willing to work with us to help solve them." What a refreshing change from the all-too-typical hard-sell approach!

I was tremendously impressed with the Oak Lane pulpit committee and their articulate chairman Terry Vrooman, who was a master of diplomacy and tact yet appropriately noncommittal. Even so I felt an instant bond with Terry that grew deeper with each visit.

We talked for a little while longer, and then the committee took Margie and me to a restaurant called Casa Conti for a late but delicious lunch. The conversation continued on a lighter note around the large table in the private dining room they had reserved. After that we followed their three cars to Oak Lane, where we were taken on a tour of the church, the neighborhood, and the manse.

It was four o'clock by the time we said goodbye that afternoon. We had met as strangers; we parted as friends. Something had clicked. It was like falling in love. There is a feeling of excitement when you think you have met that certain someone. That is what was missing in Lancaster.

What made it even more exciting for me was that Margie was feeling the same excitement, but in her characteristically sensitive way, she waited until I had expressed my feelings before sharing hers with me. "After all," she said, "you're the one who has to feel called. And wherever you go, that's where I'll want to go, too."

"But we're in this together, Margie, and the fact that you're excited, too, makes me all the more excited!"

At the same time, I did not want to become *too* excited, lest I run ahead of the Holy Spirit. What if the Oak Lane committee were to call me? How would I know if God wanted me to accept? What if they decided they were not interested in me? After all, they said they were talking with other candidates. While they were very friendly, they were also judiciously non-committal. I prayed fervently that night and the next day, as I had so many times before when facing a major faith decision, that God would make it abundantly clear what I should do. I wanted to be ready and willing to go anywhere God wanted me to go, do anything God wanted me to do. I prayed God would help me not to be anxious, but simply to relax about it and let it happen. What a precious gift to have a partner like Margie with whom to share my innermost feelings. Our discussions helped to keep things in proper perspective.

One thing was sure: the next move was up to the committee. The move came in the form of a telephone call the following night from Terry Vrooman, who asked if I would be able to meet with the committee the following Sunday night, March 23. "We need more time to talk about some of the things we weren't able to cover with you yesterday, Dick." I readily accepted Terry's invitation to join them for dinner at the home of one of the committee members, Betty Bauer, whom I discovered was a fantastic cook and a most gracious hostess. She was known to the committee as Bucket Seat Betty, because of her admiration for the bucket seats in one of the other committee member's sports car.

That evening turned out to be one of the most beautiful faith-sharing experiences of my life as the committee members expressed their love for their church and shared their hopes and dreams for its future. I was inspired by their faith and commitment, and they seemed pleased with my responses to their questions about my vision of what a church should be and my intended style of ministry. I had the feeling the relationship was gelling, and it felt wonderful! I was wishing all along that Margie could have been with me, but she had felt she needed to stay home with the children.

Near the end of the meeting, Terry Vrooman informed me that the committee wanted to hear me preach again. I immediately interpreted that as a sign of uncertainty on the part of at least some of the committee members. I was quickly reassured, however, when Terry went on to explain that the committee had promised the congregation that they would not present any candidate whom they had not heard preach at least twice. As we were parting, Betty Bauer made a very encouraging comment, but Terry Vrooman was still noncommittal. Always the diplomat, he wanted to be sure every member of the committee would have an opportunity to voice her or his opinion after I had gone. He said he would be in touch with me when he had arranged another place for me to preach. That they wanted to hear me again was all the encouragement I needed.

I took the cloud route home that night. I was in love! But I remember how I felt when I was courting Margie. I did not want to declare myself until I was sure she felt the same way about me. I would never want to marry someone who did not love me, no matter how much I loved her. That night on the way back to Princeton my heart was telling me that Oak Lane was the place for me, *if* they wanted me.

Margie had long since gone to bed when I got home, but she had insisted that I wake her. She wanted to know in detail how the evening had gone. I was happy to comply with her wish, for I was nearly bursting with excitement and I wanted to tell her everything.

The next day we celebrated Ellen's ninth birthday, and it was not until after she and the other children had gone to bed that night that we were able to continue our discussion. Now the big question was what to do about Lancaster. I had to be sure that I was listening to God and not to my own desires. At last I was given the insight I had been waiting for. If both churches were to call me, would it be fair to go to Lancaster, if my heart were in Oak Lane? I began to see that the very excitement I was feeling about Oak Lane was God's way of answering my prayers. God was confirming my feeling that Lancaster was not the place for me, whether or not Oak Lane eventually called me.

The following night I called chairman Dick Reese and told him as tactfully as I could that I did not feel called to Memorial Church and that they should look for someone else. We had a very warm and friendly conversation, in the course of which he asked if I had anyone else to recommend. It just so happened that I had been trading pulpit committee experiences that very afternoon with a good friend and classmate, Richard Kirk, whose maturity and ability I had come to appreciate through our mutual association with the student council. I had told Dick of my intention to decline the call to Lancaster and had suggested he look into that situation. So in response to Mr. Reese's question, I immediately gave him Dick Kirk's name. As it later turned out, Dick accepted a call to Memorial Church and served there effectively for several years, before being called to a church in Philadelphia.

There was nothing to do now but wait to hear from Terry Vrooman about when and where I was to preach again for the Oak Lane pulpit committee. A growing worry, albeit a minor one, was the fact that I still did not have a clerical robe of my own. What if the committee should invite me to candidate? What kind of an impression would I make on the congregation if I should appear in the stringy, wrinkled choir gown I had been using ever since I started preaching? It belonged to the batch of robes worn by our nontouring chapel choir, and nobody cared.

Nor did I, when I was preaching in various churches. I could not afford to be proud! Now the problem was that I could not afford a robe! We had numerous bills to pay and simply did not have the money to buy a pulpit gown. The problem was solved at least temporarily, when Dr. David Hugh Jones, who was director of music at the seminary and another one of my favorite people, one day told me I could keep the gown I had been borrowing continually. I suspected he was glad to get rid of it. Even so, I appreciated the fact that I no longer had to pick up a robe from the choir room in the basement of the chapel every time I preached. Nevertheless, I needed a decent clerical robe, and that was a worry.

The day after I called Lancaster I was given another reminder that God was still very much involved in all that was happening in my life. I received a letter in the mail, not from Mr. Vrooman, but from my former South Hall neighbor and good friend Frank Watson, who had graduated the year before. The gist of Frank's brief note was as follows:

> Dear Dick,
>
> As your time at seminary draws to a close and graduation approaches, you are probably feeling the financial pinch. If you're like me and many others you must be wondering where you're going to get the money to buy a robe.
>
> Please accept the enclosed gift and use it for that purpose. There is one condition, however: You must do the same for a student in

the class behind you next year, just as someone did for me and I have done for you.

Enclosed was a check for $100! In those days that was enough to purchase a good pulpit robe. For me it was another powerful reminder of the providence of God, whose timing is as amazing as the gifts themselves. Indeed, the timing is the miracle!

I tried to express what the gift meant to me in my thank-you letter to Frank, a man of deep faith. I was sure he would understand, and I promised him that I would pass his gift on to a worthy person in the class behind me. A year later I wrote a similar letter to Bart Leach, who, having taken a student pastorate, was on a four-year program. I hope that the chain has never been broken, and that the amount has been adjusted to meet the rising cost of clergy robes!

16

The Clapper Caper

March had always been a big birthday month in our family, with Margie's coming on the 21st, Ellen's on the 24th, mine on the 29th, and Ricky's on the 31st. My father drove up from Baltimore to spend part of the weekend with us, arriving in time for dinner on the evening before my birthday. My mother was not well enough to come with him. She had been bedridden for many months and needed round the clock nursing care. What a magnificent example of a mutually caring and loving couple my parents were. My mother had always been my father's most loyal supporter and confidante throughout his demanding coaching career, accommodating with never a complaint to his late practices and irregular schedule, attending to his every need and listening sympathetically to his concerns. Now I was seeing my dad care so lovingly for my mother throughout the years of her increasingly debilitating illness, which the doctors had termed premature arterial sclerosis. It had led to a minor heart attack in August of 1956. I went down to Baltimore to see her as often as I could, and she loved having Dad read my letters to her. They had been following our progress closely ever since we left Baltimore, and Dad and I corresponded regularly and spoke at least three or four times a week on the telephone. He had visited us frequently in Princeton, and on this particular occasion it was wonderful to be able to share my candidating experiences with him.

Honeymooners Elsie Davis Stoll and Herbert Eustace Armstrong were married on June 1, 1918, and had forty-two happy years together. They were "Else" and "Army" to each other, "Muv" and "Dad" to my brother and me, and Elsie and Herb to everyone else. I could not have asked for more devoted parents, or two I admired and respected more than I did each of them. My mother was an extremely talented and creative woman, with a great sense of humor. She was beloved by the players on all of Dad's teams, and was a caring surrogate mom to many a homesick McDonogh boy, for whom there were always homemade cookies available.

Dad left on the afternoon of the 29th, taking Ellen with him for a visit to Baltimore. I spent the rest of my birthday and much of that night studying, as usual. The following evening Terry Vrooman called to say that he had arranged for me to preach on April 13 at the Presbyterian Church of Wyncote, just north of Philadelphia. He sounded more upbeat than he had been in our previous conversations and even volunteered to tell me that the committee was excited. That was good news!

About that time I needed some good news, as Margie was involved in an automobile accident on her return from meeting Ellen at the Trenton station. No one was injured, fortunately, but the car was badly damaged. We wanted to have the bodywork done immediately so that the car would be ready for our next visit with the Oak Lane pulpit committee. Aside from the accident, I had my candidating sermon to worry about, an oral exam on the Westminster Shorter Catechism to prepare for, classes to attend, papers to write, work to do in the office, and the usual family duties to perform.

Along with everything else, the student council was embroiled in a messy situation that had ballooned into a major issue for the seminary community. It meant several days of emergency meetings with the council and with the executive committee, and conferences with Dr. Mackay. Some of the students had succumbed to springtime madness. They had performed a number of sophomoric pranks, much to the consternation of President

Mackay, who felt that such antics were entirely inappropriate during Holy Week. The final straw was the stealing of the Alexander Hall bell clapper, which for Dr. Mackay was the symbol of order on the campus. The bell signaled the start and end of every class, chapel service, and special event in the life of the seminary. The perpetrators' imaginative campus decorations were quickly removed, but whoever had stolen the clapper refused to return it, despite the pleadings of the student council. What started off as a prank had become a major source of irritation, disrupting the seminary community.

The bell clapper was missing from the tower of Alexander Hall.

The morning after the student escapade (Maundy Thursday), the fiery Scot exploded in chapel, demanding that the clapper be returned immediately and holding the student council responsible for identifying and disciplining the culprits. He ordered me and the other three officers to meet with him in his office immediately following the chapel service. I had never seen Dr. Mackay so enraged.

Nor had he cooled down very much by the time we four students entered his study. Having further vented his anger, he turned to me for a response. "I'm sorry for what happened, Dr. Mackay, but I'm sure it was meant to be only a prank. I'm embarrassed that some of our students would engage in such juvenile nonsense. But you have virtually tied our hands by what you said in chapel this morning."

"How's that?" he demanded, looking very surprised.

"You've made us a police force for the administration instead of letting us handle it ourselves. You put us in a very awkward position."

Dr. Mackay's expression instantly changed to one of concern. "Oh, my! Oh, my!" he exclaimed. "Yes, yes, yes. I see what you mean."

I assured Dr. Mackay that the student council would see that the mess was cleaned up immediately, including the silly slogans that had been written in purple paint on the roadway surrounding the main quadrangle. After we left the president's study, two of my fellow officers confided to me that they had taken part in the shenanigans. That explained why they never opened their mouths in Dr. Mackay's office. They also informed me that two of the younger faculty members were also involved. The pranks took place following a beer party.

As a public relations person, I could imagine what the impact of all this would be if the press got hold of it. Some eager-beaver reporter would love to break a story like that! We had an emergency meeting of the student council that afternoon, at which I reported on our meeting with Dr. Mackay. In my brief opening speech, I said something to this effect: "We're here to talk about what happened last night and this morning's aftermath. It's a serious situation, and it has aroused a great deal of anger. Look, I know that those who took part in the affair last night were simply having some fun. They didn't intend to hurt anybody. Unfortunately, Dr. Mackay has taken it personally. He views it as an affront to his authority. He is sorry for his outburst in chapel this morning, but he wants the clapper returned. I hate to see something like this happen in his final year as president. What do you think we should do about it?"

That precipitated a lively discussion, at the conclusion of which the student council unanimously agreed to clean up the mess. No one there admitted knowing anything about the clapper. Within a few minutes after the meeting, Fred McKirachan, the president of our senior class and by virtue of his office a member of the council, sought me out and confessed that he had been one of some thirty students who had taken part in the tomfoolery. "I had no idea Dr. Mackay would be so upset," he said looking both apologetic and concerned.

I asked Fred point blank: "Do you know who has the clapper?"

Without hesitation he told me the names of the two students, who had apparently acted on their own. They too were members of the council. They had boasted to Fred that they had stolen the clapper.

"Can you persuade them to return it?"

"I'll try."

"Tell them if they turn it over to you, there will be no questions asked."

I was hoping the students would do the right thing, without my having to confront them. I had no intention at that point of revealing to them or to anyone else that I knew they were the guilty ones, nor would I have revealed my source.

The campus was cleaned up that very afternoon. There were no classes on Good Friday, but Fred reported to me that morning that the two clapper thieves had refused to return it. "They said they would give it back when they are good and ready. They didn't like the way Dr. Mackay acted in chapel yesterday, and I guess they think they're going to teach him a lesson." Fred was obviously disgusted with their attitude and behavior.

To his credit, Dr. Mackay humbled himself before the faculty and students in chapel the following Tuesday and apologized for his outburst. He appealed to whoever had taken the clapper to return it "for the good of the entire community."

We had another meeting of the student council that afternoon. The two clapper-nappers had much to say, having no idea that I knew they were the culprits. They openly rejected every comment to the effect that the pranksters had now gone too far. Dr. Mackay had apologized for his display of temper and had appealed for those responsible now to do the right thing. By refusing to return the clapper, they were deliberately provoking the president and defying his authority. Right or wrong, to him it was a serious matter. That was reason enough to comply with his wishes. The entire council, with the exception of the two pseudo-innocents, agreed that whoever had the clapper should return it.

I had many private meetings with Dr. Mackay in the days that followed. He was beginning to run out of patience and was even talking about suspending or expelling the guilty persons, whom I learned were not in the best standing with the president for other reasons. I told him I knew who was responsible and was hoping they would voluntarily return the clapper.

I communicated Dr. Mackay's feelings to Fred and asked him to pass the word on to the recalcitrant pranksters. Despite his warnings, they refused to comply.

I needed such a problem and the extra meetings it entailed "like a hole in the head," as the saying goes, but the campus donnybrook had at least kept me from stewing about candidating on the 13th of April. When that fateful day finally arrived, I was, nevertheless, as tense as ever. The weather was perfect, and the trees and shrubs were beginning to bloom in Wyncote. The Oak Lane pulpit committee members were there en force with spouses. I preached at the eleven o'clock service, after which Margie and I and the Vroomans were guests of Russell Hanscom, another member of the committee, and his wife, Evelyn, for a scrumptious Sunday dinner and relaxing conversation at a nearby restaurant. It was 4:00 p.m. when we finally got up from the table, and nearly six o'clock when we got home. What a wonderful day!

My friend and classmate Milt Riviere stopped by later that evening to hear how the day had gone. I was bubbling with enthusiasm, as I speculated about the possibilities of being called to Oak Lane. We were sitting there talking at 10:30 p.m., when there came a knock at the door of the apartment. I went to the door, expecting to see another student, but to my amazement there, crowding into the narrow hallway, were the twelve members of the Oak Lane pulpit committee! I introduced them to Milt, who was impressed by this fantastic show of support. They had had their meeting and voted unanimously to ask me to be their candidate. They were so happy and excited about it that they had spontaneously decided to drive en masse to Princeton that very night to tell me!

After Milt graciously excused himself, I ran upstairs to wake Margie. I shook her shoulder firmly but gently, whispering, "Margie! Margie! Wake up! The pulpit committee is here!"

Our daughter, Ellen, who was sleeping in the other bed, sat up and rubbed her eyes. "What's a pulpit committee?" she asked sleepily.

"I'll tell you all about it tomorrow, Ellen. Go back to sleep."

She lay back down and closed her eyes contentedly. By then Margie was beginning to wake up. "The Pulpit Committee?"

"Yes! All twelve of them are downstairs. Throw on some clothes as quickly as you can, and come on down."

She did, and was greeted by twelve smiling faces. There were hugs all around, and not a few joyful tears. Each member of the committee had her or his own comment to make, including the hitherto reserved chairman, wary Terry Vrooman, who was bubbling with enthusiasm as he humorously reported on their meeting. He also related that in their excitement their car caravan had inadvertently made a wrong turn on the Roosevelt Boulevard, and they found themselves heading north on the southbound side of that twelve-lane divided highway! The only thing they could do was cut across the wide grassy median strip. They managed to do that without either having an accident or being apprehended by the police. Terry then concluded his remarks, saying with a broad smile on his face, "We have unanimously voted to ask you to be our candidate for pastor of the Oak Lane Presbyterian Church."

That was a moment for faith-sharing. I wanted the committee to know what I was feeling. "I've been praying that when the time came I would know in my heart that it was a call of God. Both Margie and I have been so excited about Oak Lane that I was afraid I might be listening to my own desires instead of to the Holy Spirit. But I finally concluded that the decision would be up to you, and your answer would be God's answer to us. So I am pleased and honored to be your candidate, and couldn't be more excited about it!"

We visited a little while, prayed together, and had another round of hugs. What a joyful gathering that was! Then the twelve departed, leaving Margie and me to digest the impact of what had just happened. To think that the entire committee had driven all the way to Princeton at that hour of the night to tell us the result of their meeting! Could I ever have had a more convincing invitation or a more confirming call than those beautiful people had extended? Knowing both my father and Dr. Fritsch to be night owls, I made a quick call to each of them to tell them the good news. They were delighted.

We could hardly sleep that night, and it seemed as if I had barely closed my eyes when I heard the telephone ringing downstairs. I bounded down the stairs in my pajamas thinking for sure it would be Terry Vrooman, but instead it was Bill Hervey. He was calling from the office. "Sorry to wake you, Dick, but I came in early to get some work done and I found something you need to see. You'd better get over here as fast as you can. Bring your station wagon."

When I got back upstairs, I looked at the clock and only then discovered it was 6:00 a.m. Margie woke up enough to ask me who had called and then went back to sleep. Without shaving, I threw on some clothes, and hurried out the door and down to the parking lot. In less than ten minutes from the time of Bill's call I was unlocking the front door of the Administration Building. There in the center of the lobby was a large pile of stones, and sticking conspicuously out of the top of the stone heap was— guess what?—the bell clapper!

There was a note attached. It read as follows: "'And there you shall build an altar to the Lord your God of unhewn stones; you shall lift up no iron tool upon them' (Deut 27:5)." The culprits had added insult to injury with their unseemly display, returning the missing symbol of authority and order in a manner well calculated to arouse the ire of president Mackay.

How they had managed to get the stones into the building without being discovered I shall never know. It had to be late at night when the deed was perpetrated. What they had not counted on was that someone would discover their nefarious monument and prevent it from having its intended effect.

Bill helped me load the rocks into the back of the station wagon. It was still early in the morning, and no one saw us. Even if they had, they would not have known what we were doing. Bill was not aware that I knew who the guilty students were, and I said nothing as we drove to the opposite side of the quadrangle and stopped in front of one of the entrances to Alexander Hall. Swiftly but stealthily lugging as many of the heavy stones as each of us could handle at a time, we carried them into the dormitory and down the first-floor hall to the room where the two pranksters lived as roommates. We could hear their voices and the sound of an electric shaver, which helped to prevent their hearing us, as we carefully built a high wall of stones up against their door. The whole construction was designed to come crashing into the room as soon as the door was pulled open from within.

Bill's devilish grin indicated that he appreciated the retributive justice in what we were doing. We quickly slipped out of the dormitory and disappeared before anyone saw us. Bill went back to the office and I returned to the apartment to have breakfast and get ready for classes. At eight o'clock I was able to locate the superintendent of grounds and buildings, Tom Brian, who was also in charge of campus security. Tom had been as upset as Dr. Mackay about the missing clapper, and he was gleefully appreciative of the manner of its discovery and what Bill Hervey and I had done. By 8:30 a.m. the clapper had been returned to its proper place, and Dr. Mackay was pleased that the clapper caper had finally ended. When I later told him what had happened, he thoroughly enjoyed the irony in the turn of events. "Their sins were visited upon them," he said, chuckling with delight.

I heard later that the two roommates were furious that someone had attributed the crime to them. They were totally unaware that I had discovered their identity soon after the crime. I had been hoping they would return the clapper in response to our appeals, but apparently they were enjoying the commotion they had caused. They thought they had acted in complete anonymity and had been able to get away with the campus prank of the decade. Instead, not only was their plan foiled, but the wall of stones at their door was proof that their guilt was no secret. They pressed Tom Brian to tell them who had returned the clapper but to no avail. Nor did they find out who had laid the stones at their doorstep. The erstwhile clappernappers were highly visible as they sheepishly lugged the stones out of the dormitory and hauled them away in their car.

Early that morning, after I had gone to class, Margie gave her parents a full account of our late night visit, and that evening I stopped in to see the person who had recommended me to the committee, Dr. Douglass. He too was elated to hear the news. Everyone we told was well aware, of course, that the committee was not the final authority. They had merely asked me to be their nominee for the office of pastor. The formal call had to be extended by the congregation and approved by the Presbytery of Philadelphia. There were several constitutional requirements to be met before that could happen, including my preaching to the Oak Lane congregation, being voted upon at a special congregational meeting, receiving an official call, being transferred from the Baltimore Presbytery to the Philadelphia Presbytery, appearing before the ministerial relations committee, and being examined and approved by the Philadelphia Presbytery. As far as I was concerned, however, the most important step of the actual calling process was the invitation of the pastor nominating committee for me to be their candidate.

There was also the little matter of completing the requirements for graduation from Princeton Seminary! With so much going on in my life on and off campus, I was struggling to keep up with my course assignments. One requirement I had yet to fulfill was the field education department's stipulation that every student should participate in an evening of evangelistic calling under the supervision of the pastor of a church that had an organized evangelism program. I had signed up to take part in such a program on Tuesday evening, April 15, two days after the surprise visit of the Oak Lane twelve. I drove with three other students to the First Presbyterian Church of Avenel, New Jersey, where the Rev. Charles Sherrard Mackenzie was then pastor. My three traveling companions were not at all happy about having to spend an evening in this manner. I was more curious than resentful, although I was not expecting it to be an especially worthwhile experience.

How wrong I was! That evening had a powerful and lasting impact on my ministry. What was meant to be only a onetime exposure to the evangelism program of a local congregation spawned ideas in me that eventually became the focus of and set the course for my lifelong ministry. It was not just what we did that night. It was the ideas it triggered in me for building upon what I had experienced.

Each of us students was paired with a lay member of the church, who was to be the team leader. We students were supposed to be the support persons. After receiving a set of cards and some brief instructions, we went out two by two to make our calls. My partner and I had four wonderful visits. None of the people we saw was a member of the church, but all had attended at least one worship service. I was amazed at how willing people were to invite us into their homes and to talk. My partner was a genuine "people" person. He listened, he invited, he made friends. He was compassionate, concerned, and caring.

Everyone we saw thanked us for coming, and three of the couples expressed interest in joining the church. When we got back to the church, we wrote a brief report on each card, and then all the teams reported on their calls. That was a thrilling experience, and I decided right then and there that I would want any church I served to engage in such a program. That one experience was enough to convince me that if a church reaches out to its neighbors in an inviting, caring way, people will respond and the church will grow. I resolved that evangelism and stewardship would be high on my priority list, wherever I was called to serve.

17

The Call to Oak Lane

Life continued at its usual hectic pace for the next several days. We had a number of visitors, including Don McClanen, who was becoming more like a brother to me than just a friend. We corresponded regularly, spoke frequently on the telephone, and saw each other at various FCA functions.

Betty and Len Bauer came up from Philadelphia to talk with us about decorating the manse. They could not have been more helpful, and Margie and I knew they were going to be-come very special friends in the days ahead. We talked on the tele-phone with them often. There were also frequent phone calls from Terry Vrooman and other members of the Oak Lane Presbyterian Church having to do mostly with plans for Sunday, May 4, when I would lead worship and preach my candidating sermon in the morning and speak informally at a congregational din-ner that evening. The pulpit com-mittee was working hard to prepare for the big day. They sent out a let-ter informing the church members

Betty and Len Bauer were a tremendous help to us from the very start. Len was an enthusiastic supporter and Betty was kindness personified. She and Margie became very dear friends.

about their decision, introducing my family and me, and announcing a special congregational meeting called for the purpose of acting on the committee's recommendation.

Meanwhile, back on the campus, I was struggling to find the right topic for my candidating sermon. I had no barrel or even a bucket of sermons to draw upon. I was worrying about finding time to write a sermon in the midst of everything else that was going on at the time, when providentially and ironically, my notoriously lengthy middler sermon suddenly popped into my mind as the logical choice! Its weakness suddenly became its strength, as I realized it summarized my theology and faith more than anything else I had written. That, after all, was what the congregation needed to hear from someone candidating for their pulpit. So my immediate task was to trim it down and relate it to the occasion. Recalling Dr. Macleod's pertinent question, I did not want the revised version to be too long. Having chosen my topic, I then sent all the information for the church bulletin to Terry Vrooman as he had requested.

On Sunday, April 27, the telephone rang at 7:30 a.m. It was Bart Leach reporting that he had to take his wife, Ruth, to the hospital and asking if I could preach for him in Stockton, New Jersey, that morning. I could and did. For me it was a good warm-up for the following Sunday. For Bart it was a relief. For Ruth it was a baby girl!

Two days before our big Sunday in Oak Lane, my brother and his French wife, Colette, arrived for an overnight visit. Herb had been in the U.S. on business. They drove up from Baltimore to spend a couple of days with us in Princeton. It was the first time we had seen them since they visited us in Portsmouth, Ohio, on their honeymoon. Herb and I stayed up late that Friday night catching up, and continued until they left for New York on Saturday afternoon. Not knowing when we would see each other again made the parting difficult for both of us.

There was no time for tears, however. Tomorrow was May 4, and I needed to gear up for C-Day (C for candidating). I spent the rest of the afternoon and much of the night going over my sermon and planning what I would say at the congregational dinner. Margie's parents arrived early the next morning to spend the day with our children so that Margie and I would be unencumbered while we were being put through our paces at the church.

Since the Bauers had insisted that we make their house our headquarters for the day, we went directly there, pulling into their driveway at ten o'clock. About forty minutes later I walked around the corner to the church, where Miss Alma Lee Cadell, the dynamic, septuagenarian church deaconess, was waiting to greet me. She whisked me through the Sunday school auditorium and up the stairs to the pastor's study at the end of the balcony, so that I could have a few minutes to myself. Terry Vrooman knocked on the door about five minutes before the hour and ushered me downstairs to where the rest of the pulpit committee was waiting to have a brief prayer.

Our prayers were graciously answered, for the service seemed to go well. It was a thrilling experience for me and for Margie, who greeted the congregation with me afterward. Everyone who came through the line was most cordial and made us feel right at home.

Afterwards we had a leisurely lunch at the Bauers' and spent the rest of the afternoon there. They had thoughtfully arranged for me to have some privacy so that I could prepare for the evening program. Margie took a nap while I worked on my talk. At about twenty minutes of six we all walked back to the church, where people were gathering for the congregational dinner. Margie and I recognized many of the persons we had seen that morning, and were introduced to some we had not met. At six o'clock Terry Vrooman called on elder Russell Stewart, the clerk of session, to say grace. Then we formed two lines and helped ourselves to some of the tastiest casseroles and other dishes I had ever sampled. That was our introduction to the covered-dish suppers for which, we were told, the Oak Lane Presbyterian Church was famous. The reputation was well deserved!

When everyone had finished eating and the tables were cleared, we sang some gospel songs I had never heard but thoroughly enjoyed. Terry then traced the history of the pulpit committee's eighteen-month search for a pastor and told how and why they had eventually decided on me. The congregation enjoyed his colorful description of the committee's wild ride to Princeton. He concluded his mostly humorous introduction by inviting me to speak informally about "my vision for the church" if I were to be called as their pastor.

I spoke for thirty minutes about the mission of the church, expressing my excitement about Operation Bootstrap and what they were already doing. Toward the end of my remarks I commented on the fact that there was no mention in Operation Bootstrap about evangelism. "If you want to grow, you will have to reach out to your neighbors and invite them to church."

"What do you have in mind?" someone asked.

"I'm talking about an organized visitation program. How many of you would be willing to take part in such a program?"

"Do you mean going door to door?"

"Yes, but not in a way that offends people." I went on to tell them about my experience in Avenel and what an impression it had made on me. "I'm convinced there are many unchurched people in Oak Lane who would respond to such an approach. I would really be excited about a church that was willing to do that kind of evangelism. Let me ask you again, How many of you would be willing to take part?"

Before the words were out of my mouth, hands were going up all over the place. Soon almost everyone there had a hand in the air. I was astounded by their overwhelming response. "That's wonderful!" I exclaimed. "What an exciting church this must be with that kind of commitment." Then, counting on their seeing the twinkle in my eye, I added, "If you call me as your pastor, I'm going to hold you to it!" With that I sat down.

Terry thanked me, made a few summary remarks, and then called on me for a closing prayer. By the time we had finished saying good night to everyone it was nearly nine o'clock. We stopped at the Bauers' for a brief visit and to pick up my robe, then continued on home, arriving at the apartment at 10:30 p.m. Margie's parents were as eager to hear how our day had gone as we were to hear how they had fared with our three children.

What a day it had been! My heart was full of joy as I lay in bed that night, pondering all that had happened. I felt totally at peace. There was no use worrying. I had tried to be honest and to be myself. There was nothing I could do now but wait. The rest was up to the congregation and to God. With that thought, I dropped off to a sound sleep.

The next day it rained steadily from morning until night. Our day was brightened, however, by the happy news that Margie's younger sister, Martha Sproul, had given birth to her first child, a baby girl. I had another student-council meeting that night and did not get home until 9:45. Twenty minutes later the phone rang. It was a jubilant Terry Vrooman. "The entire pulpit committee is here with me, Dick. We're calling to tell you that the congregation voted unanimously tonight to call you as their pastor!" I was holding the phone so that Margie could hear Terry. The two of us were elated. I'm sure Terry could tell how pleased and excited I was to hear the news, not because it had turned out the way I wanted, but because I knew in my heart it was a call of God.

Terry informed me that the Presbytery's Committee on Ministerial Relations, as it used to be named, wanted to know if I could meet with them on Thursday of that week at 3:30 p.m. at Presbytery House. I told Terry I would call and let them know that I could. "In the meantime," said Terry, "you and I need to decide on a date for your ordination and installation. I'll call you again tomorrow night to talk about that and some other things we need to discuss."

Since Margie and I had been invited to have dinner the next night at the home of Dr. Charles R. Erdman, I told Terry I would call him after we returned from our engagement. As soon as we hung up, I called my dad to tell him the good news. He was as thrilled as I was. There were many other people we needed to tell, and we spent many minutes on the phone telling them.

In our lengthy telephone conversation the following night, Terry and I discussed dates for the ordination and installation service. I had informed the search committee of my having promised Don McClanen that I would participate in the national FCA conference in Estes Park, Colorado, in August. I had been planning to take time off during the month of August in order to fulfill that obligation. One possibility, therefore, had been that I would be ordained and installed in late August or early September. The committee had felt that was entirely too long to wait, however, and had unanimously agreed to recommend in their report to the congregation that I begin as soon as possible, with the understanding that I be given a month's vacation in August. A man of uncommon discernment and sensitivity, Terry Vrooman had made the case that the Oak Lane Presbyterian Church was part of the larger church and was enabling me and my family to have the vacation we would otherwise have had, and that after our strenuous years at the seminary we needed and deserved some time off. While I would be working at the FCA conference, it would be a refreshing change of pace, and the travel to and from Colorado would be a relaxing and fun time for my family and me. Terry further had pointed out that I would be able to get a five-week head start on my pastoral duties in the church. The congregation had concurred with the committee's recommendation that I be installed in June and had graciously agreed to allow me to be on vacation during the month of August.

What Terry and I now had to decide, therefore, was which day in June, and could I fulfill all the Presbytery requirements by that date? We agreed to shoot for the evening of Wednesday, June 25, for the ordination and installation service, with the understanding that my family and I would move into the manse the previous week. That would give us a few days' time to get settled before I began my duties as pastor. My first day in the pulpit would be Sunday, June 29. All of this was contingent upon my fulfilling all the requirements for ordination, and upon my being approved by the ministerial relations committee and the Presbytery of Philadelphia. The call of God had to be confirmed by God's church.

The dates we had chosen put us on a very tight time schedule. There were certain steps that now had to be taken, however, beginning with my meeting with the ministerial relations committee. In the meantime, it had been raining steadily since Monday morning. Not until Thursday afternoon did we see the sun. It pierced the clouds as Margie and I were driving to Philadelphia, where I was to meet with the committee. No call could be approved by the Presbytery without the prior endorsement of the ministerial relations committee. The interview that afternoon went smoothly, and the committee spelled out for me the steps to be taken in order for me to be ordained and installed as pastor of the Oak Lane Presbyterian Church. They approved the date for my ordination and installation, subject to my passing the ordination exams. I had heard that the Philadelphia Presbytery's exams were tough, but I wanted to be ordained in Oak Lane.

The next day I wrote to the Rev. Paul Warren, chair of the committee on candidates of the Baltimore Presbytery, and explained why I had decided to be ordained in Philadelphia. According to Presbyterian polity, a minister must be installed by the calling Presbytery but may request to be ordained by his or her home Presbytery. I felt that my being ordained in Oak Lane would mean more to that congregation and to me than my being ordained in Baltimore would mean to the people at Faith Presbyterian Church. I alerted Dr. Warren that the Philadelphia Presbytery would be writing to request that my records be transferred.

As we approached the end of our final semester at Princeton Seminary, Margie and I found ourselves entertaining and being entertained frequently. Classmates came to swap candidating stories, and the people who had played a part in our call to Oak Lane, like the Fritsches and the Douglasses, wanted to hear all the details. It was hard for us to think about anything else.

There was plenty else to think about, however, with term papers coming due, final exams staring me in the face, the student council winding up its affairs, office work to keep up with, and ordination exams to prepare for. When she was not working on the invitation list to my ordination and installation service, Margie was busy typing term papers for me. She was also still working three nights a week in the medical center.

Despite the frantic pace of our lives, we managed to find time for fellowship and for special occasions. Saturday, May 17, for example, was a great day for us. Margie and I took the children with us to Philadelphia, stopping en route for lunch at Cliff's Restaurant on Route 1, one of our favorite hamburger joints. Andy went downtown on the subway with me to order my first clerical gown while Ellen and Woody accompanied their mommy to Ardmore to see the woman whose dressmaking skills Margie had called upon back in the days when we were living in Havertown. As we had agreed, Margie picked up Andy and me at the subway entrance at Broad Street and Hunting Park at 2:30 p.m. A few minutes later we arrived at the Oak Lane Presbyterian Church, where we spent the rest of the afternoon and evening enjoying the well-attended Haig Class Fair. This is an annual event sponsored by one of the women's Bible classes. It was a marvelous opportunity for us to mingle with many of the church members and for them to get acquainted with our children, who had never had so much attention.

Our children also had the opportunity to inspect what in a few weeks would be their new home, which must have seemed palatial to them after three years in our tiny seminary apartment. Margie and I were impressed and pleased with the way the manse was being spruced up for our occupancy. It was after ten o'clock by the time we got home that night.

There was only one more week of classes, to be followed by the usual examination period. After my final class on Thursday I caught a late afternoon train to New York and spent that night through Saturday morning in an FCA brainstorming and planning session with Don McClanen and a small group of interested volunteers. The movement was growing but struggling financially. I was becoming more and more involved and committed to the program, and Don seemed to value my friendship and advice. We were becoming closer all the time.

I returned from New York Saturday afternoon in time to go with Margie to a barge party with the Palmer Squares and the Suburban Squires. That was the first of what was to become an annual event involving singing groups from all over the United States, and their families. They continue to meet each year for the Spring Sing, a three-day weekend of song and merriment hosted by one or more of the groups at some appropriate venue. That first gathering was a modest beginning, but loads of fun for Margie and me, who had been associated with both the Squires and the Squares. We started from New Hope, Pennsylvania, and immediately filled the air with glorious song, as our mule-drawn barge moved slowly along the Delaware Canal. People waved and applauded from their back porches as our song-filled platform floated slowly by. Our picnic supper by the Delaware was followed by an informal but planned program, with the two groups alternating after every three or four numbers. It was a memorable evening, and none of us complained about the length of the program. Margie's parents, however, who were babysitting for us, were relieved when we finally walked in the door just before midnight.

The following Thursday, after I had transported Ellen and Andy to their respective schools, Margie and I left Woody with a babysitter and drove to Philadelphia for the day. Margie went to the local elementary school to see about enrolling Ellen and Andy for the next year. She then met a friend for lunch while I visited with Alma Lee Cadell at length at the church. Miss Cadell, as she was called by everyone, was the consummate professional church worker, and an invaluable source of information about everything and everyone. I had come loaded with lists of questions covering every aspect of the church's life and work. Having worked at the church for more than three decades, Miss Cadell was able to answer most of them or refer me to someone else who could. She was a product of the old school, having been trained at the Tennent College of Christian Education in Philadelphia as a deaconess, an office that had long since ceased to exist in the Presbyterian Church. When Tennent College finally closed its doors, its assets were transferred to Princeton Theological Seminary. Its name has been preserved in the seminary's Tennent Hall, which now houses the Department of Christian Education.

Miss Cadell was more than a beloved staff member at the Oak Lane Presbyterian Church. She had become an institution, highly revered and respected, and totally dedicated to her ministry. Our visit that day set the tone for our relationship, which was built upon mutual respect and affection, but always strictly formal. As close as we became, we were never on a first-name basis.

Margie joined us in the middle of the afternoon. Miss Cadell took an instant liking to her, and it quickly became apparent, as she accompanied us on a tour of the manse, that she intended to take our family under her wing.

Before heading back to Princeton, we called on Betty Bauer. We were having a pleasant visit, when she suddenly surprised us by handing me a beautifully wrapped package. "It's a graduation present from the pulpit committee," she said, and then invited me to open it right then and there. It was a handsome clock, which Margie was as pleased to receive as I was.

Once again we had much to share with each other on the way home. We stopped at Cliff's again for hamburgers, and they tasted better than ever!

18

Goodbye, Princeton—
Hello, Philadelphia!

The next several days were filled with closures of various kinds: the last meeting of the student council, at which I turned over the gavel to my newly elected successor; Margie's last night as a file clerk at the medical center; my last term paper turned in; my last exam taken; the president's farewell reception for the 1958 graduates; the baccalaureate service; the annual alumni/ae banquet; graduation; saying goodbye to many friends.

The week of graduation was especially busy for Margie, as well as for me. On top of everything else we had lots of company, including an overnight visit from Don McClanen, for some lengthy and intense conversation about the FCA; Dora and Phil Quanbeck, who were back for Phil to receive his PhD degree at commencement; and my father, who came for my graduation. The night before, Dad and I had one of our wonderful marathon talks, which never lacked for subject matter. We two night owls would continue long after everyone else had gone to bed, much to Margie's consternation; she worried when I stayed up too late. It took her a few years to accept the fact that I could get by on six hours sleep at night. In that respect I took after my father.

Friday, June 6, dawned bright and beautiful. It was one of those perfect days that James Russell Lowell wrote about, "when Heaven tries the earth, if it be in tune," just right for our graduation exercises in the beautiful Princeton University Chapel, where Margie and I had been married on a wintry day more than ten and a half years before. Never had I thought, when I escorted Margie back down the aisle, or when I sat as an undergraduate in those same wooden pews, that I would one day be standing on the chancel steps to receive a degree from Princeton Theological Seminary.

Margie's parents were there for the impressive ceremony, of course, along with my dad, Maurice and Irene Armstrong, Ed and Ruth Emack, and other relatives and friends. Some stayed for the buffet luncheon in the seminary dining hall afterward. The cameras were constantly clicking, as the graduates bade one another farewell. It was one of those sad-happy times that always leave me a bit depressed.

My father was the last of our family and friends to leave, and no sooner had he driven out of sight than I turned to the task of preparing for my ordination exams. The Philadelphia Presbytery had a reputation for giving tough examinations, which one of my classmates had taken and failed on the first try. His experience did not help my confidence one bit. I did not know what to expect, except that the exams would take all day and cover the theological waterfront. For the next four days I spent every spare hour reviewing three years of lecture and class notes, rereading my term papers, and boning up on my Greek and Hebrew. I had crammed so much information into my head that I wondered whether I would be able to retrieve any of it when I needed it.

I was still cramming early Wednesday morning, June 11, as I drove the sixty-five miles or so to the First Presbyterian Church of Wayne, Pennsylvania, where Dr. John Galloway, chair of the candidates committee of the Philadelphia Presbytery, would administer the exams. Within ten minutes of my arrival at the church I was seated at a large table in one of the classrooms at the church, reading the first exam question. Except for an hour lunch break I remained seated at that table the rest of the day. It was an exhausting but surprisingly enjoyable experience, and I left the church feeling confident that I had passed.

When I got home that evening, Margie first inquired about the exams and then informed me happily that she had finished addressing and mailing all of the invitations to the ordination and installation service. That was a major accomplishment on her part and a huge relief to me! But there was still the rest of the packing to be done in preparation for our move to Oak

Lane the following week. Margie and I worked late every night packing and labeling boxes.

Friday, June 13, was my last day at the development office, where I had worked for nearly three years. Joe MacCarroll, Bill Hervey, and the rest of the office staff surprised me with a little farewell reception at the end of the day. It was hard to say goodbye to those friends and colleagues I had worked with so closely and compatibly. Sentimental soul that I am, as I walked out the door of the administration building, my thoughts drifted back to that incredible visit in Dr. Mackay's office. It seemed so long ago, and yet how swiftly the years had passed!

That night and the rest of the weekend we packed and packed and packed. On Monday morning we took a carload of our belongings to Oak Lane, arriving at the manse about noon. After unloading the boxes, we continued on to Wayne, where a smiling John Galloway reported that I had passed all the ordination exams. Oh, happy day! From there we drove into Philadelphia so that I could stop by the Presbytery office to drop off the finalized details of my ordination and installation service. I was working on a very tight time schedule, inasmuch as I was to appear before the Presbytery the very next day! Assuming I was approved for ordination, my call to Oak Lane could then be acted upon. It was after five o'clock when we finally arrived at the apartment, having accomplished a great deal on that busy Monday.

That night there came a knock at the door, and when I opened it, I was greeted by a burst of beautiful harmony. In walked the entire group of Palmer Squares, singing all the while! This was their regular rehearsal night, and I already had said farewell to them at a previous meeting. But here they were, having come to present me with a couple of farewell gifts. One was a beautifully framed copy of a poem titled, "Ode to the Choreographer, or What Are You Going to Do on Monday Nights from Now On?" The title was a humorous reference to my constant harping on the importance of choreography, and the poem was facetiously sentimental. I would indeed miss those Monday night rehearsals, plus the performances and the rich fellowship I had enjoyed with the Squares, not to mention the sheer pleasure of the singing itself. As an all-male, close-harmony group, we had achieved a high degree of musical excellence. Despite all the joking and laughter, I am sure the group could tell that Margie and I were deeply touched by their show of friendship and support. Our three children listened in wide-eyed wonder, as I joined the Squares for a few more songs before they departed. What a beautiful ending to a wonderful day!

It was hard to sleep that night, with so much on my mind. Intermingled with the jubilation of the Squares' visit was some anxiety about my appearance before the Philadelphia Presbytery the next morning. Knowing I had to leave very early, I slept only fitfully, waking up frequently to look at the clock. Somehow my personal sandman has never taught me to trust an alarm clock when I have to make an early morning departure. The result was that I was on my way to Springfield, Pennsylvania, where the meeting was to take place, well ahead of my planned departure time, and I arrived at the church with plenty of time to spare. Terry Vrooman and John Fowler showed up later to represent the Oak Lane congregation.

In keeping with Presbyterian polity, I was there to read my statement of faith and to be examined orally by the Presbytery. Once I was approved for ordination, the call of the Oak Lane Presbyterian Church would then be presented for Presbytery's approval, and I would be asked to present my plans for the service of ordination and installation. The candidates committee had approved the final version of my faith statement, although I myself was not too pleased with the somewhat stilted language I had ended up using. It sounded too much like an exposition of the Apostles' Creed, but it was "orthodox," and that is what the committee wanted. Since I did believe what I had written, I was not inclined to quibble with them about the language.

When my turn to be examined finally came, I read my statement from the podium and then waited for the commissioners to respond. The first question came quickly. One of the commissioners observed that I had not mentioned the communion of saints and asked me if I believed in it. I said I did, and that was that. There were no other questions. Somebody moved that the examination be sustained and that I be approved for ordination. I was then asked to leave the sanctuary while the motion was discussed and voted upon. I had hardly made it to the narthex, when I was called back into the sanctuary and informed that I had been approved for ordination. I was then asked to present my plans for the service, and after receiving Presbytery's approval I walked back to the narthex, where Terry and John were waiting to offer their congratulations.

We had been standing there only a minute or two when the moderator announced over the public-address system, "Will Mr. Armstrong please return to the podium!"

As I quickly reentered the sanctuary and headed down the aisle to the moderator's podium, I was wondering what could possibly have gone wrong. Were my papers not in order? Or what? My anxiety was instantly displaced by embarrassment, when the moderator's voiced boomed over the PA system, "I think you picked up my agenda by mistake. We can't go on without it!"

Several hundred commissioners instantly erupted with loud laughter, as I was making my way down the aisle. Sure enough, there in my folder were the moderator's agenda and other official papers relating to the business of the day! The laughter continued, as I handed the agitated gentleman his papers and returned to my seat. My introduction to the Philadelphia Presbytery was memorable but hardly auspicious!

After spending most of the day at Presbytery, I returned to Princeton in time for supper, following which Margie and I plunged into our packing chores with a vengeance. Margie's father worked with us until after midnight, when the last box was finally tied and labeled. Without his help we might have been working all night. As it was, we collapsed into bed about 1:30 a.m. Neither of us got very much sleep on our last night in the apartment that had been our home for three happy years.

A few hours later we were up and dressed again. Our long-awaited moving day had finally arrived! Wednesday, June 18, had been circled on our big calendar in the kitchen for many weeks, to remind us to be ready. Margie and I were frantically scurrying about, when the big moving van turned into the driveway in front of our dormitory at about 8:30 a.m. The time of our departure had arrived!

Dr. Childs came by a few minutes later to pick up Woody for the day. Ellen and Andy had left earlier in the carpool for their last day of school, after which they were to go to their grandparents' house. The movers had already loaded the things that had been in storage since we moved from Baltimore. They never expected it to take them most of the day to pack the contents of our little apartment, but it did! What space there was in those few rooms was well filled. Margie and I were cleaning behind the men, as each room became empty. We were working nonstop all day, except for a brief time-out for lunch with our entryway neighbors, Ann and Griff Matthews.

When the movers had finished and the van had finally pulled away at 5:00 p.m., we spent another hour scrubbing and dusting. After a last-minute inspection, we paused for a moment for one last nostalgic look, and then closed the door behind us.

Having stopped by 106 Broadmead to say goodbye to the Childses and to our children, who were remaining with their grandparents in Princeton, we drove directly to Oak Lane, arriving at the manse at exactly seven o'clock. Betty Bauer came by a few minutes later with a big box containing a full-course roast chicken dinner. Did it taste good!

Thirty minutes later the moving van pulled up, and the hard-working crew of four went immediately to work. John Fowler arrived on the scene shortly thereafter and was a tremendous help directing traffic inside our spacious new home. There was plenty of room to spare in the three-story, seven-bedroom manse, for all our belongings! It was after midnight when the crew completed their unloading. Having made up the bed in our new bedroom, Margie and I collapsed into bed at 1:00 a.m.

The next morning we started early and worked full speed all day and well into the night. Despite numerous but brief interruptions from parishioners stopping by to welcome us, we were amazed at how much we were able to accomplish. Margie called her parents to let them know our telephone had been installed, to give them a progress report, and to check on Ellen, Andy, and Woody.

The next day we returned to Princeton to pick up the children, had lunch at Cliff's on the way back, and returned to the staggering task of unpacking, deciding where to put everything, shifting furniture, hanging pictures, and all the other chores relating to moving into a new home. Even the children were up late that night, as we worked on their rooms.

The next day, Saturday, we were at it again. There were, of course, more interruptions, all pleasant, including visits and phone calls from more parishioners and friends, but we again worked late and accomplished much. On Sunday morning we drove to the Neshaminy Warwick Presbyterian Church, where our friend Frank Watson was pastor. Since I had not yet been installed at Oak Lane, we felt we should worship elsewhere. After a pleasant lunch with the Watsons, we returned home and spent the rest of the afternoon and evening working at the manse.

On Monday the first of two shipments of furniture arrived from Asheville, North Carolina, where our good friend Dick Gordon and his father had bought and were operating a furniture factory. As a special graduation and ordination present they had overwhelmed us by letting us select a dining-room suite and a living-room suite months before from their new catalogue. The beautifully designed and newly manufactured pieces arrived on Monday and Tuesday, just in time for us to have them in place for the dinner that Margie was hosting Wednesday evening for the participants in the ordination and installation service, their spouses, Margie's parents, my father, my aunts Nora and Edith Stoll, and my brother Herb, who was able to return unexpectedly for the occasion.

Wednesday, June 25, was, to Margie's dismay, hot and humid. But at least it was not raining, and her dinner was enjoyed by all of our guests, who found it hard to believe that we had been in the manse for less than a week. The worship service that night was inspirational from start to finish. The sanctuary was filled to capacity, with as many visitors as members, including friends from Philadelphia, Baltimore, Princeton, and even Portsmouth. The Palmer Squares were there in force and delighted everyone by singing several numbers at the reception following the service. My Old Testament professor and adviser, Charles Fritsch, preached the sermon, and my cousin Maurice Armstrong gave the prayer of ordination. One of my two most vivid memories of the service was the feeling that my neck was going to snap from all the weight on my head during the laying on of hands.

The other strong memory was the thrill of putting on my new robe and being escorted by the moderator to the pulpit, where, after thanking the people, I pronounced my first benediction as an ordained minister of the gospel. As I looked out at the faces of the people, I sensed that I had been called by God into the ministry and to this place.

June 25, 1958. The Rev. Dr. Charles T. Fritsch and the Rev. Dr. Maurice W. Armstrong, two key figures in my pilgrimage of faith, are en route from the manse to the church for the installation service. In addition to Hebrew I took several electives under Prof. Fritch, who enlightened and excited me about preaching from the Old Testament. My cousin Maurice was the person who steered me to Princeton Seminary. He had been and continued to be my pastoral counselor and confidante. I was so pleased that both of them could participate in my ordination/installation service.

Goodbye, Princeton—Hello, Philadelphia!

One last pose before the service. Two hours later I would have that "Rev." Dr. Bodo had warned me about in front of my name! It was an awesome feeling to know that my long-awaited ordination was about to take place and I would be installed as pastor of the Oak Lane Presbyterian Church!

Despite the heat and humidity, the reception was as exhilarating as the service was inspiring. The receiving line seemed to go on forever, as Margie and I exchanged greetings with all the friends and church members who had come. We were still greeting people when my father, brother, and aunts left to drive back to Baltimore. It was after eleven o'clock by the time the last people had gone and Len Bauer was turning out the lights. I lay in bed that night savoring the afterglow of all that had happened. Our honeymoon with the Oak Lane Presbyterian Church had begun!

Margie's parents left after breakfast the next morning, having spent the night at the manse. Margie then got busy again opening boxes and putting things away, while I spent most of the day organizing my study at the church. After supper I helped Margie unpack more boxes, and by late that night we had washed and put away the entire contents of the last two barrels of chinaware.

Throughout these hectic days I had been stealing time here and there to work on my sermon and plan the worship service for my first Sunday in the pulpit. That day arrived in a hurry, and in some ways was every bit as exciting as the Wednesday night service had been. Never could I have guessed what lay in store for me and the congregation I had been called to serve. Nor could I have anticipated the kinds of challenges I would have to face and the skills I would need to meet them. Within a few days I had encountered all kinds of situations and taken on responsibilities for which I had received no preparation whatsoever in seminary. What I had acquired, however, was a sound theology, a solid devotional life, and an awareness of my total dependence on the God who had called me into ministry, all of which compensated for my lack of experience.

Like every new pastor, I had to go through all the customary "firsts"— my first baptism, my first communion, my first wedding, my first funeral, my first board meeting, my first daily vacation Bible school, my first everything. The orientation to parish ministry does not take long in a solo pastorate, however, and within a few weeks a new pastor has usually seen and done it all.

I certainly had by the time those first five weeks had rushed by. How well I remember my first experience with the daily vacation Bible school. As I was leading a hundred squirming children and their teachers in the group singing during the opening exercises, I was inwardly laughing and saying to myself, "What if the boys in the press box could see me now!"

The Oak Lane Presbyterian Church

Visitors are always impressed by the beauty of the sanctuary.

One of the huge Tiffany stained-glass windows that enhance the worshipful ambiance of the sanctuary.

As a newly ordained minister I knew I had much to learn, and as the Rev. Dr. Raymon Kistler, who had been the interim minister, said in his charge to the congregation, "He doesn't have a barrel of sermons to draw upon!"

Top: "The Manse" at 6635 N. 11th St., Philadelphia, PA, seemed palatial to us after three years in our tiny seminary apartment. Our children were thrilled to have their own individual rooms. **Bottom**: Margie stood beside me to greet the congregation on the night of my installation and she continued to do so from then on, symbolizing our togetherness in ministry and our closeness as a couple.

Epilogue

A Sense of Being Called

That was the beginning of our ten wonderful years in Oak Lane. I have chronicled the circumstances and events leading to and including the call to my first pastorate. I wish there were space to include the names of the many other persons whose lives intertwined with ours en route from the press box to the pulpit. Lest the story become too lengthy, I have had to omit many people and experiences I should like to have included.

One highlight I must mention was the birth of our fifth child, Elsie Stoll Armstrong. There was much rejoicing in the congregation on the arrival of the first baby in the Oak Lane manse in many decades. And it was a great joy for our family to welcome the namesake of my mother, whose death had occurred less than three weeks earlier. How often these two traumatic reminders of our continuity and our mortality, birth and death, are bracketed in the experience of families. We were glad that my mother was out of her misery at last, but sorry that she did not live to see the little girl who would bear her name.

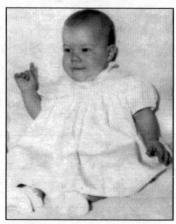

November 1960. Meet Elsie Stoll Armstrong, our Oak Lane baby, who would one day become a Presbyterian minister like her daddy.

A Sense of Being Called

There were many incidents in the life of the church that were important but not relevant to this story, the focus of which is the experience of being called by God. Although I have omitted much, I have tried to provide sufficient detail to show that the call of God is an ongoing affair. In my case, the affair did not end with my Damascus Road experience. That was only the beginning. The sense of being called and the awareness of God's providential guidance were present throughout my seminary years and have continued ever since. The call of God has always been dynamic, never static. The manifestations of it have come in various and sundry ways, and at varying intervals, while the confirmation has always had a retroactive perspective and a widely fluctuating impact. The purpose and direction of the call have been clearer at some times than they have been at other times.

There have been some difficult decisions along the way, choices to make when I was not sure whether God was calling me to go or to stay. In every case, however, subsequent events have confirmed my sense of being called, and I can understand what the Apostle Paul meant when he declared that "in everything God works for good with those who love God, those who are called according to God's purpose" (Romans 8:28, RSV). What a comfort to know that even if the worldly wise think otherwise, God honors our decisions when we have striven to the best of our ability to discern and to do God's will.

As I write this, I can look up from my desk and see on the walls around me photographs of times past. Many of them are visible reminders of my pilgrimage of faith and of the miraculous ways God has been and continues to be at work in my life. Even more important, as I think about the days ahead and all that I hope yet to do, they remind me how totally dependent I am on the grace of God and how grateful I should continually be for a sense of being called.